O'Nelleo

LITERARY SOCIETIES FOR BOOKMEN

A collection of Societies, Clubs and
Periodicals in England and America,
relating to literature and the arts

Compiled by
Roger & Judith Sheppard

 TRIGON PRESS: BECKENHAM, KENT

Cover: *Charlotte Brontë (1816-55) Age 34*

First published in 1979
ISBN 0 904929 13 2
© Trigon Press 1979

All rights reserved. No part of this publication may be reproduced, stored in a retrieval system, or transmitted, in any form or by any means, electronic, mechanical, photocopying, recording or otherwise, without the prior permission of the publishers. Such permission, if granted, is subject to a fee, depending on the nature of the use.

Typeset by Tek-Art Ltd., London S.E.20
Printed and bound by Galliard (Printers) Ltd., Great Yarmouth

CONTENTS

	Page
Literary Societies	5
Book Clubs	75
Literary Periodicals & Trade Journals	77
Author and Subject Classification	79

Books published by **Trigon Press:**

SHEPPARD, R. & J.	The International Directory of Book Collectors (cloth & paperback)
POWYS, T.F.	Mr. Tasker's Gods
HUNTER, William	The Novels & Stories of T.F. Powys

Forthcoming titles:

TRIGON EDITORS	Publishing Your First Book
SHEPPARD, S.	The Worth Carols
POWYS, T.F.	Mark Only
SHEPPARD, R.	Science Fiction: Traders Handbook
TIMLIN, W.M.	The Ship That Sailed To Mars
SHEPPARD, R. & J.	Crime & Detective Fiction: a Handbook

Acknowledgements

The illustrations of Charlotte Brontë, William Shakespeare, Francis Bacon, Elizabeth and Robert Browning, Lewis Carroll, John Keats, Thomas More and Richard III are by permission of the National Portrait Gallery. John Cowper Powys by permission of E.E. Bissell. Edgar Allen Poe by permission of the American Antiquarian Society. The engravings of Charles Dickens, Samuel Johnson, John Locke and John Milton are from compilers' own collection.

Notice
Whilst every care has been taken in the compilation of this handbook, the publishers regret that they can accept no responsibility for the authenticity of the Societies listed or the accuracy of any information pertaining to them.

LITERARY SOCIETIES

ACADEMY OF COMIC ART, FANS & COLLECTORS (see under **Comic**)

ACADEMY OF COMIC BOOK COLLECTORS (see under **Comic**)

ALCOTT:

LOUISA MAY ALCOTT MEMORIAL SOCIETY
c/o Mrs. Whitney Smith, Ridge Road, Concord, Mass. 01742, U.S.A. *Membership*: 57

FRIENDS OF THE ALCOTTS
c/o Jayne Gordon, Director, Orchard House, Box 343, Concord, Mass. 01742, U.S.A. *Membership*: c.50 Society started in fall of 1978, membership open

ALGER:

HORATIO ALGER SOCIETY
4907 Allison Drive, Lansing, Mich. 48910, U.S.A. *President*: Jerry Friedland *Hon. Sec.*: Carl T. Hartmann *Publications*: The Newsboy, newsletter, 12 p.a. *Membership*: 250 Members in: England, Japan, Iran, Canada & Germany. Membership is available to any person interested in the life, times and writings of Horatio Alger Jr. *Enquiries*: Carl T. Hartmann, at above address

AMATEUR & SMALL PRESSES:

AMERICAN AMATEUR PRESS ASSOCIATION
c/o Leland M. Hawes, 5009 Dickens Avenue, Tampa 9, Florida, U.S.A. No additional information supplied *Enquiries*: The Secetary, at above address

NEW ENGLAND SMALL PRESS ASSOCIATION
45 Hillcrest Place, Amherst, Mass. 01002, U.S.A. *President & Treasurer*: William R. Darling *Vice Pres. & Clerk*: Diane Kirchkow *Publications*: Newsletter, 6 p.a.; annual catalogue; occasional anthologies; Readers' Agency *Membership*: 220 *Enquiries*: Wm R. Darling, at above address

AMATEUR & SMALL PRESSES cont'd.

UNITED AMATEUR PRESS ASSOCIATION

315 Clinton Street, Findlay, Ohio, U.S.A. No information given on structure, publications or activities. *Enquiries*: William Ellis, Secretary, at above address

AMERICAN ANTIQUARIAN SOCIETY (see under **Antiquities**)

AMERICAN COUNCIL FOR LEARNED SOCIETIES (see **Eighteenth Century: AMSECS**)

AMERICAN PRINTING HISTORY ASSOCIATION (see under **Printing**)

AMERICAN SOCIETY FOR 18th CENTURY STUDIES (see under **Eighteenth**)

AMERICAN SOCIETY OF BOOKPLATE COLLECTORS & DESIGNERS (see under **Bookplates/Ex Libris**)

AMERICAN TEILHARD DE CHARDIN ASSOCIATION (see under **Teilhard**)

AMPERSAND CLUB of Minneapolis & St. Paul

3329-20th Ave. S., Minneapolis, Minn. 55407, U.S.A. *Committee*: Harold Kittleson, Paul Hillestad, Fred Phelps *Publications*: No newsletter; 2 books published. An informal group, limited to about 35, all local residents. *Enquiries*: J. Harold Kittleson at above address

ANCIENT MONUMENTS SOCIETY (see under **Antiquities**)

ANTIQUARIAN BOOKSELLERS' ASSOCIATION OF AMERICA, INC. (See under **Booksellers**)

ANTIQUITIES/ANTIQUES:

AMERICAN ANTIQUARIAN SOCIETY

185 Salisbury Street, Worcester, Mass. 01609, U.S.A. *President*: John Jeppson, 2nd *Director/Librarian*: Marcus Allen McCorison *Publications*: Newsletter, Jan. & June annually; books on bibliographical subjects *Proceedings*: October & April annually *Membership*: 350 honorary and by election. Subscriptions to 'Proceedings' are available; address the Editor at above address

ANCIENT MONUMENTS SOCIETY

St. Andrew by the Wardrobe, Queen Victoria Street, London, E.C.4. *President*: Rt. Hon. the Earl of Rosse, CBE, MA, LLD, MRIA, FSA *Chairman*: Ivor Bulmer-Thomas, MA, FSA *Secretary*: Matthew Saunders, BA *Membership Sec.*: Mrs. Susan Gold, BA *Publications*: 2 Newsletters, one Transactions p.a. *Membership*: 2,000 The Society is concerned with the study and the conservation of historic buildings of all ages and types and is recognised as a National Amenity Society. Our Transactions cover all aspects of architectural history, especially vernacular architecture and churches *Enquiries*: Mrs. Susan Gold, at above address

SOCIETY OF ANTIQUARIES OF LONDON
Burlington House, Piccadilly, London W1V 0HS *President*: A.R. Dufty, CBE *Hon. Sec.*: Dr. I.H. Longworth *Director*: Prof. J.D. Evans, FBA *Treasurer*: R.M. Robbins *Publications*: Antiquaries Journal, 2 p.a.; Archaeologia, occasional monographs *Membership*: 1,400 elected Fellows *Enquiries*: to above address

THE CLASSICAL ASSOCIATION
Department of Classics, University College, P.O. Box 95, Cardiff CF1 1XA *Joint Sec.*: Dr. John Percival *Publications*: Some journals published *Enquiries*: General enquiries about classical antiquity can be answered by post, or advice given about other sources of information

OXFORD ANTIQUE COLLECTORS CLUB
Hon. Sec.: Mrs. M. Poskitt, 20 Flemings Road, Woodstock, Oxon. No information supplied on structure or publications

ARCANE ORDER
Studio of Contemplation, 5340 Weller Avenue, Jacksonville, Fla. 32211, U.S.A. *Preceptor*: Dell Lebo *Vice Pres.*: Randel Dean Drake *Corresponding Sec.*: Dr. Omer Lucifer *Other officers*: Harriet Smith, John Sulik, Leonard J. Mather, William Noe, Cricket Noe *Publications*: irregular Newsletter *Membership*: 1010 *Enquiries*: Dr. O. Lucifer, Le Ranche de l'Aumade Haute, Saint-Paul-en-Forêt, 83440, Fayence, France

ARCHIVES: SOCIETY OF ARCHIVISTS
County Record Office, County Hall, Hertford. No information given on structure or publications *Enquiries*: The Secretary, at above address

ARLIS: ART LIBRARIES SOCIETY
c/o ARLIS Secretary: Gillian Varley, Kingston Polytechnic, Knights Park, Kingston, Surrey *Chairman*: Philip Pacey *Hon. Sec.*: Gillian Varley *Treasurer*: Colin Ball *Publications*: 6 News-sheets p.a.; 4 Journals p.a. *Membership*: 300+ *Enquiries*: Katherine Baird, Mem-

ARLIS cont'd.
bership Secretary, The Library, St. Martins School of Art, 109 Charing Cross Road, London WC2H 0DU

ARTHUR:

INTERNATIONAL ARTHURIAN SOCIETY

Bennett Hall, Box 12, Univ. of Pennsylvania, Philadelphia 4, Pa., U.S.A. *Secretary/Treasurer*: William Roach. No further information available on structure publications or activities *Enquiries*: Sec., at above address

ARTHURIAN SOCIETY (INTERNATIONAL)

c/o *British Branch Secretary*: Dr. Angus J. Kennedy, French Dept., University of Glasgow, Glasgow G12 8QQ *International Secretary*: Professor C. Foulon. 4 rue des Gantelles, 35 Rennes, France *Publications*: Bibliographical bulletin of International Arthurian Society, annually; copies from Prof. C.E. Pickford, French Dept., University of Hull *Membership*: 200 *Notes*: aims: to promote the study of and research into medieval Arthurian literature; international meetings held every three years, British meetings annually

ASLIB

3 Belgrave Square, London SW1X 8PL *President*: Sir Alastair Pilkington *Director-General*: Basil Saunders, MA, F.I.P.R. *Head of Information Division*: Miss S.M. Remington, ALAA *Publications*: Aslib Information, 12 p.a.; Aslib Proceedings, 12 p.a. *Organisational membership*: 1800 *Personal membership*: 300 *Scope & purpose*: To promote the efficient management and exploitation of information resources in all fields including industry, government, education and the professions *Enquiries*: Membership Secretary, at above address

ASSOCIATES OF THE UNIVERSITY OF VIRGINIA LIBRARY (see under **Friends**)

ASSOCIATION FOR SCOTTISH LITERARY STUDIES (see under **Scottish Interest**)

ASSOCIATION OF YORKSHIRE BOOKMEN (see under **Books/Collecting**)

ASSOCIATION INTERNATIONALE DE BIBLIOPHILIE (see under **Bibliophily**)

ASSOCIATION INTERNATIONALE FUTURIBLES (see under **Future**)

ATHENAEUM:

THE ATHENAEUM OF PHILADELPHIA
219 S. Sixth Street, Philadelphia, Pa. 19106, U.S.A. *President*: George Vaux *Secretary & Librarian*: Roger W. Moss, Jr. *Publications*: Athenaeum Annotations, 4 p.a.; several books each year *Membership*: 1,000 The Athenaeum is an independent research library specializing in 19thC. Anglo-American cultural history. Extensive rare book holdings *Enquiries*: Dr. Moss, at above address

AUCHINLECK BOSWELL SOCIETY (see under **Boswell**)

AUDUBON ARTISTS INC.
1083 Fifth Avenue, New York, NY 10028, U.S.A. *President*: Domenico Facci *Hon. Sec.*: Therese Censor *Treasurer*: Alice Gross *Publications*: Newsletter/catalogue of annual exhibition, 1 p.a., Jan/Feb. *Membership*: 413 *Enquiries*: Sec., at above address

AUSTEN:
JANE AUSTEN SOCIETY
Ivalls, Bentworth, Alton, Hants. *President*: The Lord David Cecil, C.H. *Hon. Sec.*: Sir Hugh Smiley, Bt. *Publications*: Annual Report of the Society; Jane Austen in Bath (J. Freeman) *Membership*: 1,700 *Enquiries*: Sir Hugh Smiley, Bt., at above address

AUTHORS:
THE SOCIETY OF AUTHORS
84 Drayton Gardens, London SW10 9SD *President*: Sir Victor Pritchett, CBE *Chairman*: Peter Dickinson *General Secretary*: David Machin *Deputy General Secretary*: Philippa MacLiesh *Assistant General Sec.*: Ian Rowland-Hill *Publications*: Newsletter — The Author, 4 p.a. *Aims*: To promote the interests of authors and defend their rights whenever and wherever they are challenged; a unique detailed contract-vetting service is provided for members. Subsidiary organizations within the membership having their own rules of admission: The Broadcasting Group, The Educational Writers' Group, The Children's Writers' Group, The Translators' Association. No extra subscription required for these organizations *Enquiries*: to above address

AUTHORS' CLUB
1 Whitehall Place, London, S.W.1. No information given on structure, publications or activities *Enquiries*: The Secretary, at above address

CHILDREN'S WRITERS' GROUP (see **Society of Authors**)

AUTHORS cont'd.

CIVIL SERVICE AUTHORS' SOCIETY
16 Palmerston Road, Twickenham, Middlesex *Hon. Sec.*: Miss Betty Richards   No information given on structure, publications or activities *Enquiries*: Hon. Sec., at above address

CRIME WRITER'S ASSOCIATION
Chairman: Margaret Yorke, Oriel Cottage, High Street, Long Crendon, Bucks. HP18 9AL *Secretary*: Marion Babson, 42 Trinity Court, Gray's Inn Road, London WC1 8JZ *Publications*: Monthly pub. 'Red Herrings', editor/PRO Martin Russell, The Lupins, The Green, Catsfield, Battle, East Sussex *Membership*: 450 Applicants have to have had published a book, or a number of stories or articles, or a play performed on television, stage or radio. Monthly meetings are held at the Press Club, 76 Shoe Lane, London E.C.4. Each year the Association awards Gold and Silver daggers for the best crime fiction and non-fiction and the John Creasey Memorial Prize for the best first crime novel *Enquiries*: The Secretary

EDUCATIONAL WRITERS' GROUP (see **Society of Authors**)

INTERNATIONAL P.E.N.
7 Dilke Street, London SW3 4JE *International President*: Mario Vargas Llosa *International Secretary*: Peter Elstob *Administrative Secretary*: Elizabeth Paterson *Publications*: Bulletin of Selected Books *Membership*: 8,000 at 76 World Centres *Enquiries*: Admin. Sec., at above address

MYSTERY WRITERS OF AMERICA, INC.
105 E. 19 St., New York, NY 10003, U.S.A. *President*: Lillian de la Torre *Executive Secretary*: Gloria Amoury *Executive Vice-President*: Hillary Waugh *Treasurer*: Jean Francis Webb *Secretary*: Joyce Harrington *Publications*: Newsletter — The Third Degree, 10 p.a. *Membership*: 800-900 *Enquiries*: Gloria Amoury, at above address

PENMAN CLUB
175 Pall Mall, Leigh-on-Sea, Essex SS9 1RE *General Secretary*: Leonard G. Stubbs, FRSA *Membership*: over 5,500, open to all writers, published or not, in any country. No further information given on structure, publications or activities *Enquiries*: Gen. Sec., at above address

Francis Bacon (1561-1626)

STOWARZYSZENIE AUTOROW ZAIKS (Soc. of Authors Zaiks)
2 Hipoteczna Street, 00-092 Warsaw, Poland *President*: Karol Malcuzynski *General Manager*: Witold Kolodziejski *Publications*: Periodical 'Wiadomosci Zaiks-U' (News of Zaiks) *Membership*: 3,919 *Enquiries*: Soc. of Authors Zaiks, 00-950 Warsaw, Hipoteczna 2, Poland

WEST COUNTRY WRITERS' ASSOCIATION
The Cottage, Nr. Stoke Gifford, Bristol BS12 6PT *President*: Christopher Fry, FRSL *Chairman*: Rev. J. Rowlands, BSc *Hon. Sec.*: Ann Manning *Publications*: W.C.W.A. Newsletter, 4 p.a.; Annual congress (May, 3 days) on Literature in the West Country *Enquiries*: Hon. Sec., at above address

BACON:

FRANCIS BACON SOCIETY
Canonbury Tower, Islington, London N.1. *President*: Comdr. G.M. Pares, RN (Ret'd) *Chairman*: N.B. Fermor *Hon. Sec.*: Mrs. D. Bramels, 12 Nevern Square, London, S.W.5. *Hon. Treas.*: T.D. Bokenham *Publications*: 'Baconiana' and Newsletter to members, periodically (usually 1 p.a.) *Membership*: c.200 *Enquiries*: The Sec., at above address

FRANCIS BACON FOUNDATION INC.
655 North Dartmouth Avenue, Claremont, California, U.S.A. *President*: Elizabeth S. Wrigley *Note*: Not a literary society, but a

BACON cont'd.

non-profit charitable and educational organisation incorporated under the laws of the State of Calif. in 1938. It maintains and operates a rare book research library on the campus of Claremont Colleges with which it is affiliated; it also makes grants to Claremont Colleges for Visiting Professors and Lecturers

BAKER STREET: (see under **Sherlock Holmes**)

THE BAKER STREET IRREGULARS

STRANGE OLD BOOK COLLECTORS

BALTIMORE BIBLIOPHILES (see under **Bibliophily**)

BAUM: (see under **Wizard**)

BERLINER BIBLIOPHILEN ABEND: (see under **Bibliophily**)

BERLINER TYPOGRAPHISCHE GESELLSCHAFT: (see under **Printing/Typography**)

BIBLIOGRAPHY: (see also **Bibliophily**)

THE BIBLIOGRAPHICAL SOCIETY

British Academy, Burlington House, Piccadilly, London W1V 0NS *President & Chairman*: A.R.A. Hobson *Joint Hon. Secs.*: R.J. Roberts, Mrs. M.M.Foot *Publications*: The Library, 4 p.a.; annual monographs *Membership*: 1,150 *Enquiries*: Mrs. M.M. Foot, The British Library, Great Russell Street, London WC1B 3DG

BIRMINGHAM BIBLIOGRAPHICAL SOCIETY

c/o Main Library, University of Birmingham, PO Box 363, Birmingham B15 2TT *President*: vacant *Secretary*: Mrs. A.M. Cadman *Publications*: informal newsletter, annual programme; working papers of the West Midlands Book Trade Project (No. 1-4 pub. 1975-8, details in Brit. national bibliography) *Membership*: c. 60, *Note*: Meetings: 6-7 evening meetings, 2 summer excursions Aims: To promote and encourage bibliographical and allied studies; to promote friendly intercourse among booklovers and scholars and to further their common interests; to hold meetings and exhibitions *Enquiries*: Hon. Sec., at above address

CAMBRIDGE BIBLIOGRAPHICAL SOCIETY

c/o The University Library, West Road, Cambridge *President*: J.C.T. Oates, FBA *Hon. Sec.*: F.R. Collieson, 23 Neville Road, Cambridge *Hon. Treas.*: W.A. Noblett *Publications*: Transactions of the Cambridge Bibliog. Soc., annually, normally in Dec.; monographs on a wide range of bibliographical topics appear at irregular intervals, at least one every five years *Membership*: c. 450, open; fee covers cost of Transactions & Monographs; *Note*: Society aims: to encourage the study of bibliography by means of publication, meetings for the presentation and discussion of papers and visits to libraries; meetings: 2 p.a., and AGM, plus visits to private libraries *Enquiries*: Treasurer, at above address

EDINBURGH BIBLIOGRAPHICAL SOCIETY
c/o National Library of Scotland, Edinburgh 1, Scotland *President*: Dr. R. Donaldson *Hon. Sec.*: I.C. Cunningham *Hon. Treasurer*: J.M. Pinkerton *Publications*: Transactions of the Edinburgh Bibliographical Society, in theory annual, but recently rather irregular *Membership*: c. 250, equally split between institutions and individuals *Note*: Aims are to promote the discussion of bibliog. matters (concerning printed books & mss) esp. Scottish and to publish Transactions and other relevant works. Meetings: generally 6, held in Edinburgh from Oct. to March *Enquiries*: Hon. Sec. at above address. Soc. cannot provide any sort of reference service; enquiries relating to Scottish bibliography should be addressed to the Nat. Library of Scotland

LIVERPOOL BIBLIOGRAPHICAL SOCIETY
Sydney Jones Library, P.O. Box 123, Liverpool L69 3DA *President*: Dr. J. Pinsent *Hon. Sec.*: M.R. Perkin *Publications*: News-sheet (annual, not published, distributed to members only); Members' Exhibition, cat. 1975; The antiquarian bookseller and his Customer (cat. of a Member's exhibition, 1976) Proposed: individual surveys, reports, etc. towards a final Dictionary of the book trade in the North West *Membership*: mailing list c. 80, subscribing members, c. 30, open *Note*: Soc. was formed in 1970 as a forum for study and enjoyment of all matters relating to the ms or printed book, esp. in this region, to hold meetings, arrange visits and to publish *Enquiries*: Hon. Sec., at above address

OXFORD BIBLIOGRAPHICAL SOCIETY
Bodleian Library, Oxford, OX1 3BG *President*: Ian G. Philip *Hon. Treasurer*: Mrs. Gwen Hampshire *Publications*: Substantial mono-

BIBLIOGRAPHY cont'd.

graphs every two or three years and smaller works, 'Occasional Publications', at more frequent intervals *Membership*: c. 550, open *Note*: Society founded in 1923 to encourage bibliographical research programme of lectures and visits every year *Enquiries*: Hon. Treas. at above address

WELSH BIBLIOGRAPHICAL SOCIETY

c/o The National Library of Wales, Aberystwyth, Dyfed SY23 3BU *President*: Dr. E.D. Jones, CBE, BA, FSA, FLA *Chairman*: Rev. G.M. Roberts, MA *Hon. Sec.*: B. Jones, FLA *Publications*: The Journal of the Society, published irregularly *Membership*: 170 *Enquiries*: The Secretary, at above address

THE BIBLIOGRAPHICAL SOCIETY OF AMERICA

P.O. Box 397, Grand Central Station, New York, NY 10017, U.S.A. *President*: Thomas R. Adams *Exec. Sec.*: Caroline F. Schimme *Publications*: The Papers of the Bibliographical Society of America 4 p.a. *Membership*: 1,540 *Enquiries*: Membership Secreatry, at above address

BIBLIOGRAPHICAL SOCIETY OF CANADA

32 Lowther Avenue, Toronto, Ontario, Canada *President*: Dr. David M. Hayne *Sec. & Treasurer*: Mrs. R.C. Jacobsen *Membership*: 350 No further information available on structure or publication *Enquiries*: The Secretary, at above address

BIBLIOGRAPHICAL SOCIETY OF AUSTRALIA & NEW ZEALAND

18 Oakes Street, Cook. A.C.T. 2614, Australia *President*: Dietrich Borchardt *Hon. Sec.*: Victor Crittenden *Publications*: Newsletter – 'Bulletin', 2 p.a. Editor: Dr. Brian McMullin *Membership*: 150 *Enquiries*: The Sec., at above address

THE BOTETOURT BIBLIOGRAPHICAL SOCIETY

College of William and Mary, Williamsburg, Va. 23185, U.S.A. *Chairman*: Prof. Robert Maccubbin, English Dept. *Committee*: A.Z. Freeman, Sarah V. Gray, David C. Jenkins, Cecil M. McCulley, Gary A. Smith, John L. McKnight, Thaddeus W. Tate *Publications*: Programs for fall & spring, and occasional pamphlets on colonial

Virginia libraries *Membership*: 97 *Enquiries*: Prof. Maccubbin, at above address

BIBLIOGRAPHICAL SOCIETY OF THE UNIVERSITY OF VIRGINIA

Alderman Library, Charlottesville, Va. 22901, U.S.A. *President*: Irby B. Cauthen, Jr. *Sec./Treasurer*: Ray W. Frantz, Jr. *Publications*: Studies in Bibliography, annual, ed. Fredson Bowers *Membership*: 1,000 *Note*: International Society, founded 1947, of bibliographers, book collectors, librarians, scholars and others interested in books and bibliographies. Convention/Meeting: annual, Charlottesville *Enquiries*: The Secretary, at above address

INTER-AMERICAN BIBLIOGRAPHICAL & LIBRARY ASSOCIATION

Box 600583, North Miami Beach, Florida 33160, U.S.A. *President*: A. Curtis Wilgus *Sec./Treasurer*: Magdalen M. Pando *Publications*: Doors to Latin America, 4 p.a., Jan./April/July/Oct. *Note*: A.C. Wilgus compiles 'Door to Latin America', a bibliographical listing of recent books and pamphlets on Latin America *Enquiries*: Sec., at above address

BIBLIOPHILEN GESELLSCHAFT IN KOELN (see under **Bibliophily**)

BIBLIOPHILY: (see also **Bibliography** and **Books/Collecting** and **Friends**)

BALTIMORE BIBLIOPHILES

Evergreen House, 4545 North Charles Street, Baltimore, Maryland 21210, U.S.A. *Notes*: no information received on publications, membership or activities *Enquiries*: *Secretary*: Ms. Elizabeth Baer, at above address

PITTSBURGH BIBLIOPHILES

Hunt Botanical Library, Carnegie-Mellon University, Pittsburgh, Pa. 15213, U.S.A. *Chairman*: Joseph Molnar *Publications*: annual Yearbook and other books *Membership*: 250 *Enquiries*: Hunt Botanical Library at above address

SOCIETY OF BIBLIOPHILES

54 Fordham Court, Albany, NY 12209, U.S.A. *President*: Wayne Somers *Chairman*: Mort Grant *Treasurer*: Edwin Gilcher *Note*: No information given on publications, membership or activities *Enquiries*: The Secretary, at above address

BIBLIOGRAPHY cont'd

SOCIETY OF JEWISH BIBLIOPHILES (see under **Jewish Interest**)

THE PHILOBIBLON CLUB

Philadelphia, Pa., U.S.A. *Honorary Presidents*: Lessing J. Rosenwald, Robert E. Spiller *President*: George R. Allen *Vice Pres.*: Howell J. Heaney, David A. Fraser *Treasurer*: Howard H. Lewis *Secretary*: Thomas M. Whitehead *Publications*: Selected talks, latest: Ernst Schulz's The Study of Incunables, 1977 *Note*: Founded in 1893, the Club consists of book collectors, librarians, booksellers and others interested in the history of the book, book collecting, publishing and authors. Meetings with speakers once a month, Oct. to May *Enquiries*: The Sec., Temple University Libraries, Philadelphia, Pa. 19122, U.S.A.

ASSOCIATION INTERNATIONALE DE BIBLIOPHILIE

Siege Social: Bibliothéque Nationale, 58 rue de Richelieu, 75084 Paris Cedex 02, France *President*: Frederick B. Adams *General Sec.*: Jacques Guignard, Conservateur en chef de la Bibliothéque de l'Arsenal, 1 rue de Sully, 75004 Paris, France *Publications*: Newsletter — Le Bulletin du Bibliophilie, 4 p.a. *Membership*: 430 *Enquiries*: M. Guignard, Secrétaire général, as above

BERLINER BIBLIOPHILEN ABEND

Marburger Strasse 3, 1000 Berlin 30, Germany *President*: Erich Barthelmes *Secretary*: Horst Behrend, Heydenstrasse 21, 1000 Berlin 33, Germany *Membership*: 30 *Enquiries*: Sec., at above address

BIBLIOPHILEN GESELLSCHAFT IN KOELN

Trajanstrasse 19, P.O. Box 250, 407 D-5000 Koeln 1, West Germany *President & Chairman*: Hanns-Theo Schmitz-Otto *Publications*: Newsletter — Wandelhalle der Bucherfreunde, 4 p.a. *Membership*: 480 *Note*: No further information supplied *Enquiries*: to above address

FRAENKISCHE BIBLIOPHILENGESELLSCHAFT e.V.

Sitz Bamberg, Leithe 1, D-8600 Bamberg-Bug. W. Germany *Vorsitzender*: Dipl. Ing. Hans Sendner *2.Vorsitzender*: A.M. Kolb *Schatzmeister*: Hans Simon *Publications*: Newsletter — Mitteillungen, 2 p.a. 'Wandelhalle der Buecherfreunde', 4 p.a. *Enquiries*: Hans Sendner, at above address

GESELLSCHAFT DER BUCKERFREUNDE ZU HAMBURG e.V.
Poseldorferweg 34, D-2000 Hamburg 13, W. Germany *President*:
C. Egmont Hagedorn *Hon. Sec.*: Dr. jur. Gerhard Commichau
Other officers: Gilbert Krauel, Hans Kurig, Hellmut Saucke *Publications*: Newsletter/Circular: 2 p.a. *Membership*: 180 *Enquiries*: C. Egmont Hagedorn, at above address

LE LIVRE CONTEMPORAIN et BIBLIOPHILES FRANCO-SUISSES
72 Av. Henri Martin, 75116 Paris, France *President*: M. Felix Benoit Cattin *Treasurer*: M. Claude Fay *Membership*: 150 *Enquiries*: M. Benoit Cattin, 4 Place Deufert Rochereau, 75014 Paris, France

SOCIÉTÉ DES BIBLIOPHILES BELGES SÉANT À MONS
Maison Losseau, 37 rue de Nimy, 7000 Mons, Belgique *President*: André Dufrane *Chairman*: Maurice Arnould *Hon. Sec.*: Christiane Pierard *Other officers*: Félix Francart, Robert Tondreau *Publications*: Publications de la Société des Bibliophiles, in 8° (no. 1 à 45); in 4° (no. 1-3), c. 1 per 3 years *Membership*: limited to 50 nominative members + 15 societies *Note*: Founded 1835. Texts about history of Mons & Hainault. Studies about mss, incunabula stored in the Library of Mons or elsewhere *Enquiries*: to above address

SOCIÉTÉ DES BIBLIOPHILES DE GUYENNE
3 rue Mably, 33075 Bordeaux Cedex, France *President*: Raymond Darricau, professeur à l'Universite de Bordeaux III *Hon. Sec.*: Charles Teisseyre, agrégé de l'Université *Publications*: Revue Française d'Histoire de Livre, trimestrielle *Membership*: 1,000 *Enquiries*: to above address

SOCIÉTÉ ROYALE DES BIBLIOPHILES ET ICONOPHILES DE BELGIQUE
4 boulevard de l'Empereur, 1000 Bruxelles, Belgium *President*: Charles Vander Elst *Hon. Sec.*: Georges Colin *Other officers*: Eugène Rouir, Administrateur-Trésorier *Publication*: Le livre et l'estampe, trimestrielle *Enquiries*: Eugène Rouir, avenue du Forum, 25 (Bte 18), 1020 Bruxelles, Belgium

BIRMINGHAM BIBLIOGRAPHICAL SOCIETY (see under **Bibliography**)

BOOKS/COLLECTING (see also **Bibliography** and **Friends**)

ASSOCIATION OF HANDCRAFT PRINTERS (see under **Printing/Typography**)

ASSOCIATION OF YORKSHIRE BOOKMEN
Hon. Secretary: Miss W.M. Heap, 28 Crawshaw Road, Pudsey, LS28 7UB *Note*: No further information given on structure, publications, membership or activities *Enquiries:* Hon. Sec., at above address

THE BOOK CLUB OF CALIFORNIA
312 Sutter Street, Room 510, San Franciso, Ca. 94108, U.S.A. *President*: Mr. Muir Dawson *Exec. Director*: Gaye L. Kelly *Publications*: Quarterly News-Letter *Membership*: 1,000 *Enquiries*: to above address

BOOK CLUB OF DETROIT
c/o Robert C. Thomas, Gale Research Company, Book Tower, Detroit, Mich. 48230, U.S.A. *Sec. & Treasurer*: Robert H. Thompson *Membership*: 75 *Note*: No further information given on structure, publications or activities *Enquiries*: to above address

BOOK COLLECTORS' SOCIETY OF AUSTRALIA
64 Young Street, Cremorne, N.S.W. 2090, Australia *President*: Walter W. Stone *Treasurer*: Mrs. N. Johnson *Publications*: Newsletter — Biblionews, 4 p.a. *Membership*: 306 *Enquiries*: Walter W. Stone, at above address

THE BOOK-HUNTER'S SOCIETY
Tarland House, Baxhall Road, Tunbridge Wells, Kent *Chairman*: Dr. A.O. Chick *Hon. Sec.*: Mrs. Mary Woodruffe *Publications*: Newsletter — Journal and Chronology, 1 p.a. *Membership*: new society — initially 39 members *Enquiries*: Mrs. Mary Woodruffe, 3 Rustwick, Rusthall, Tunbridge Wells, Kent

CAMBRIDGE PROFESSIONAL BOOK ASSOCIATION
Chairman: Geoff Green, 132 Boxworth End, Swavesey, Cambridge CB4 5RA *Treasurer*: Lyn Chatterton, c/o Cambridge University Press, Trumpington Street, Cambridge CB2 1RP *Secretary*: Gilmour Drummond, c/o Woodhead Faulkner, 8 Market Passage, Cambridge CB2 3PF

FORENING FOR BOGHAANDVÆRK
Norre Farimagsgade 74, 1, 1364 Copenhagen K, Denmark *Chairman*: Austin Grandjean *Hon. Sec.*: Vibeke Schultz *Publications*: Periodical — Bogvennen, yearbook *Membership*: 2,300 *Enquiries*: Hon. Sec., at above address

GUILD OF BOOK WORKERS
1059 Third Avenue, New York, NY 10021, U.S.A. *President*: Mary C. Schlosser *Hon. Sec.*: Grady E. Jensen *Vice Pres. & Membership Chairman*: Jeanne F. Lewisohn *Vice Pres. at Large*: Gale Herrick *Publications*: 4 Newsletters p.a.; 3 Journals p.a. *Membership*: 300 *Note*: Aims to keep alive craft of hand book production from calligraphy to fine binding. Membership comprises hand binders, restorers, illuminators, calligraphers, decorated paper makers, librarians and collectors interested in these fields *Enquiries*: to above address

LONG ISLAND BOOK COLLECTORS
at Adelphi University Libraries, Garden City, NY 11530, U.S.A. *Note*: No information given on structure, publications, membership or activities *Enquiries*: The Director, at above address

MAXIMILIAN-GESELLSCHAFT
2 Hamburg 13, Magdalenenstrasse 8, B.R.D. *President*: Dr. Ernst L. Hauswedell *Hon. Sec.*: Reinhold Busch *Other officers*: Prof. Dr. Paul Raabe, Director Wolfenbuttel Library *Publications*: Newsletter — Philobiblon, 4 p.a. *Membership*: 1,100 *Enquiries*: to above address

NATIONAL BOOK LEAGUE
7 Albermarle Street, London W1X 4BB *President*: The Lord Goodman, CH *Chairman*: Simon Hornby *Immediate Past Chairman*: Michael Holroyd *Hon. Treasurer*: Ian Norrie *Deputy Chairman*: Margaret Drabble *Publications*: Newsletter: Booknews, 4 p.a. *Membership*: 4,100 *Enquiries*: Ivor Courtney, Secretary, at above address

OXFORD BOOK ASSOCIATION
1 The Avenue, Kennington, Oxford *Patron*: Sir Basil Blackwell *Chairman*: Andrew Ivett *Hon. Sec.*: Harry Knights *Publications*: irregular newsletter *Membership*: 180 *Enquiries*: Harry Knights, at above address

BOOK COLLECTING cont'd.

PRIVATE LIBRARIES ASSOCIATION

16 Brampton Grove, Kenton, Harrow, Middlesex, HA3 8LG *President*: Douglas Cleverdon *Chairman*: David Chambers *Honorary Secretary*: Frank Broomhead *Publications*: 'The Private Library', 4 p.a.; 'News Letter' and 'Exchange List', 4 p.a.; Members' Annual Volume *Membership*: 1,000 *Notes*: An international society of book collectors. Also under the aegis of PLA are: Society of Private Printers (see under Printing/Typography) and Bookplate Society (see under Bookplates/Ex Libris) *Enquiries*: Hon. Membership Sec., John Allison, 5 Criffel Avenue, Streatham Hill, London SW2 4AY

ROXBURGHE CLUB

Loxbeech, Mount Street, Battle, East Sussex TN33 0JY *President*: The Duke of Northumberland, KG, PC, DCL, FRS *Vice-Pres.*: The Viscount De L'Isle, VC, KG, PC, GCMG, GCVO *Hon. Treasurer*: Philip L. Bradfer-Lawrence, MC *Hon. Secretary*: Christopher Dobson, CBE *Publications*: Privately printed books are produced by the Club from time to time; and Members print books privately under the Rules for presentation to all Members *Membership*: 40 *Enquiries*: Hon. Sec., at above address

BOOK CLUB OF CALIFORNIA (see under **Books/Collecting**)

BOOK CLUB OF DETROIT (see under **Books/Collecting**)

BOOK COLLECTORS' SOCIETY OF AUSTRALIA (see under **Books/Collecting**)

BOOK HUNTERS' SOCIETY (see under **Books/Collecting**)

FORENING FOR BOGHAANDVÆK (see under **Books/Collecting**)

BOOKPLATES/EX LIBRIS:

BOOKPLATE SOCIETY

under aegis of P.L.A. *President*: Peter G. Summers *Chairman*: Philip C Beddingham *Honorary Secretary*: Prof. W.E. Butler, 9 Lyndale Avenue, London NW2 2QD *Publications*: Newsletter, 4 p.a.; occasional monographs *Membership*: 200 *Enquiries*: Prof. Butler, at above address

AMERICAN SOCIETY OF BOOKPLATE COLLECTORS AND DESIGNERS

1206 North Stoneman Avenue, No. 15, Alhambra, Ca. 91801, U.S.A. *Director & Editor*: **Audrey Spencer Arellanes** *Publications*:

Bookplates in the News, quarterly newsletter; annual Yearbook *Membership*: 200 *Note*: annual membership fee includes both publications *Enquiries*: The Editor, at above address

DEUTSCHE EXLIBRIS-GESELLSCHAFT e.V.
Vorsitzender (Präsident): Paul G. Becker, Reckenberger Str. 65, D-4830 Gütersloh 1, W. Germany *Sekretär (Geschäftsstelle)*: Hans Kruse, Schauenburger Str. 100, D-2300 Kiel 1, Germany *2. Vorsitzender*: Karl Heinz Wichmann *Schriftleiter des Jahrbuches*: Norbert Ott *Schatzmeisterin*: Margot Wichmann *Publications*: Jarhbuch für Exlibriskunst und Graphik; 'Mitteilungen' der Deutschen Exlibris-Gesellschaft *Membership*: 250 *Enquiries*: to above address

BOOKSELLERS:
BOOKSELLERS ASSOCIATION OF GREAT BRITAIN & IRELAND
154 Buckingham Palace Road, London SW1W 9TZ *President*: J. May *Director*: G.R. Davies *Publications*: Bookselling News, 6 p.a. (to members only) *Membership*: 3,150 *Enquiries*: M.J. Bedford, at above address

ANTIQUARIAN BOOKSELLERS' ASSOCIATION OF AMERICA, INC.
50 Rockefeller Plaza, New York, NY 10020, U.S.A. *President*: Laurence Witten *Vice President*: John H. Jenkins *Secretary*: Elisabeth Woodburn *Treasurer*: Harvey W. Brewer *Membership*: 740 *Enquiries*: Ms. Janice M. Farina, Administrative Assistant, at above address

BOSTON: THE BOSTONIAN SOCIETY
Old State House, 206 Washington Street, Boston, Mass. 02109, U.S.A. *President*: William B. Osgood *Director*: Thomas W. Parker *Clerk*: Roger Allan Moore *Publications*: Proceedings, newsletter, 1 p.a. *Membership*: 1,300 *Enquiries*: Mary Leen, Librarian, at above address

BOSWELL: THE AUCHINLECK BOSWELL SOCIETY
131 Main Street, Auchinleck, Ayrshire, KA19 2AF, Scotland Proprietors of the Auchinleck Boswell Museum & Mausoleum, Kirk Brae, Auchinleck, Ayrshire *Hon. Chairman*: J. Peterson, Founder Member *Hon. Vice Chairman*: Mrs. P.S. Boswell *Hon. Sec. & Treas.*: Gordon P. Hoyle, Founder Member *Publications*: Newsletter, 2 p.a., to members only *Note*: To promote interest and to collect donations of Boswelliana in any form, i.e. ancient documents, books, china,

Elizabeth Barrett Browning (1806-61) Age 52

BOSWELL cont'd.
furniture, jewellery, coins relating to the Boswells, esp. to James Boswell, the Biographer. Also to research into the Boswell families from 1504 to present day. Annual dinner held in Aug. Lit. Soc. parties most welcome by appointment *Enquiries*: Gordon P. Hoyle, at above address

BOTETOURT BIBLIOGRAPHICAL SOCIETY (see under **Bibliography**)
BRITISH CARTOGRAPHIC SOCIETY (see under **Cartography**)
BRITISH FANTASY SOCIETY (see under **Fantasy/S.F.**)
BRITISH MENSA SOCIETY (see under **Mensa**)
BRITISH PRINTING SOCIETY (see under **Printing/Typography**)
BRITISH THEATRE ASSOCIATION (see under **Theatre**)
BROADCASTING: THE BROADCASTING GROUP (see **Soc. of Authors**)

BRONTË:

THE BRONTË SOCIETY
Brontë Parsonage Museum, Haworth, Keighley, West Yorks. BD22 8DR *President*: Margaret Lane, MA, Countess of Huntingdon *Chairman*: Mrs. Jocelyn Kellett, B.Comm. *Hon. Sec.*: Albert H. Preston *Hon. Editor*: Charles H. Lemon *Publications*: Transactions, newsletter 1 p.a. (Nov.) *Membership*: 2,100 *Enquiries*: Membership Sec., at above address

BRONTË SOCIETY
Shaw Road, Long Pasture Road, Little Compton, Rhode Island

*Robert Browning (1812-89)
Age 46*

02837, U.S.A. *Membership*: 1,500 *Note*: No information given on structure, publications or activities *Enquiries*: The Secretary, at above address

BROWNING:

THE BROWNING SOCIETY OF LONDON

9 Lakenheath, Southgate, London N14 4RJ *President*: Mrs. Elaine Baly *Hon. Acting Secretary & Treasurer*: Roy E. Bolton *Publications*: Browning Society Notes, 3 p.a. *Membership*: c. 75, open *Note*: a Society to promote the works of Robert Browning & Elizabeth Barrett Browning, and others and to collect and exchange items of lit. & biog. interest. Meetings: four or five p.a. *Enquiries*: R.E. Bolton, at above address

BROWNING INSTITUTE

P.O. Box 2983, Grand Central Station, New York, NY 10017, U.S.A. *Membership*: 450 *Note*: No information given on structure, publications or activities *Enquiries*: The Secretary at above address

NEW YORK BROWNING SOCIETY

P.O. Box 2983, Grand Central Station, NY 10017, U.S.A. *Publications*: Yearbook *Membership*: 46 *Note*: No further information given on Society *Enquiries*: The Treasurer, at above address

BURNS:

BURNS FEDERATION

Dick Institute, Elmbank Avenue, Kilmarnock, KA1 3BU *President &*

BURNS cont'd.

Chairman: Albert W. Finlayson *Hon. Sec.*: J.F.T. Thomson *Senior Vice Pres.*: S.K. Gaw *Jnr. Vice Pres.*: Mrs. M. Rennie *Schools Competitions*: James Glass *Publications*: Burns Chronicle, 1 p.a.; quarterly bulletin to members *Membership*: 346 clubs whose members total over 36,000 *Enquiries*: Hon. Sec., at above address

BURNS SOCIETY OF THE CITY OF NEW YORK
c/o St. Andrews Society, 281 Park Avenue South, New York, NY 10010, U.S.A. *Membership*: 200 *Note*: No information supplied on structure, publications or activities *Enquiries*: The Secretary, at above address

BURROUGHS:

THE BURROUGHS BIBLIOPHILES
6657 Locust, Kansas City, Mo. 64131, U.S.A. *Editor & Founder*: Vern Coriell *Chairman*: Clarence (Bob) Hyde *Vice Pres.*: Stanleigh B. Vinson *Treasurer*: William Thailing *Publications*: The Burroughs Bulletin; The Gridley Wave *Membership*: 2,500 *Enquiries*: Vern Coriell, at above address

EDGAR RICE BURROUGHS — FRIENDS OF ERB—DOM
Rt. 2, Box 119, Clinton, LA. 70722, U.S.A. *President*: C.E. Cazedessus Jr. *Hon. Sec.*: Mrs. C.E. Cazedessus Jr. *Publications*: ERB—dom Magazine, 5 p.a. *Membership*: figure not given *Enquiries*: ERB—dom at above address

BYRON:

THE BYRON SOCIETY
Byron House, 6 Gertrude Street, London SW10 0JN *President*: The Earl of Lytton, OBE *Hon. Director*: Mrs. Elma Dangerfield, OBE *Joint Chairmen*: William St. Clair/Ian Scott-Kilvert, OBE *Vice Presidents include*: John Murray, CBE/Peter Quennell *Publications*: The Byron Journal, an annual journal *Membership*: over 1,000 *Enquiries*: Hon. Director, at above address

CABELL:

THE JAMES BRANCH CABELL SOCIETY
665 Lotus Avenue, Oradell, New Jersey 07649, U.S.A. *President*: James N. Hall *Hon. Sec.*: Paul Spencer *Publications*: Newsletter — Kalki-Studies in James Branch Cabell, 4 p.a. *Membership*: 300

Lewis Carroll (Rev Charles Lutwidge Dodgson) (1832-98)

Enquiries: Paul Spencer, at above address

CALIFORNIA: THE BOOK CLUB OF CALIFORNIA (see under **Books/Collecting**)

CALLIGRAPHY:

GUILD OF BOOKWORKERS (see under **Books/Collecting**)

SOCIETY FOR ITALIC HANDWRITING
69 Arlington Road, London, N.W.1. *Editor*: A.S. Osley *Publications*: Journal of the Society, 4 p.a. *Membership*: 2,000 *Enquiries*: Society for Italic Handwriting, at above address

SOCIETY OF SCRIBES AND ILLUMINATORS
43 Earlham Street, London WC2H 9LD *Chairman*: Ieuan Rees *Hon. Sec.*: Mrs. Sue Cavendish *Publications*: S.S.I. Newsletter, 3 p.a.; occasional circular for urgent announcements *Membership*: 900 *Enquiries*: G.R. Fleuss, Membership Secretary, 26 Teversham Drift, Cherry Hinton, Cambridge CB1 3JX

CAMBRIDGE BIBLIOGRAPHICAL SOCIETY (see under **Bibliography**)
CAMBRIDGE PROFESSIONAL BOOK ASSOCIATION (see under **Books/Collecting**)

CARROLL:

THE LEWIS CARROLL SOCIETY
c/o Edward Wakeling, Hon. Secretary, 36 Bradgers Hill Road, Luton, Beds. LU2 7EL *President*: Ellis Hillman *Chairman*: Marion Waller *Hon. Sec.*: Edward Wakeling *Treasurer*: John N.S. Davis *Membership*

CARROLL cont'd.

Secretary: Lindsay Fulcher *Publications*: Jabberwocky, the Journal of the L.C.S., 4 p.a.; Bandersnatch, Newsletter, 4 p.a. *Membership*: 320 *Note*: Aims and objectives: to promote interest and research into life and works of the Revd. Charles L. Dodgson (Lewis Carroll) *Enquiries*: Hon. Sec., at above address

CARTOGRAPHY:
BRITISH CARTOGTAPHIC SOCIETY

Warren Farm, Sherfield English, Romsey, Hants. SO5 0FQ *President*: Ian A.G. Kinniburgh *Hon. Sec.*: John H.C. Wilks *Hon. Treasurer*: P.S. Hodson *Publications*: 4 Newsletters, 2 Journals p.a. *Membership*: figure not given *Enquiries*: Hon. Sec., at above address

CATHER:
WILLA CATHER PIONEER MEMORIAL AND EDUCATIONAL FOUNDATION

Red Cloud, Nebraska 68970, U.S.A. *Chairman of the Board*: Mildred R. Bennett *President*: Viola S. Borton *Publications*: WCPMEF Newsletter, 4 p.a. *Membership*: 1,000 *Enquiries*: c/o Viola S. Borton, at above address

CATHOLIC LIBRARY ASSOCIATION
461 W. Lancaster Avenue, Haverford, Pa. 19041, U.S.A. *President*: Sister Franz Lang, O.P. 1979-81 *Executive Director*: Matthew R. Wilt *Vice President*: Kelly Fitzpatrick *Publications*: Catholic Library World, 10 p.a. *Membership*: 3,284 *Enquiries*: Matthew R. Wilt at above address

CAXTON CLUB
60 West Walton Street, Chicago, Ill. 60610, U.S.A. *President*: Arthur H. Miller, Jr. *Hon. Sec.*: Richard R. Seidel *Vice President*: Frank O. Williams *Membership*: 250 *Note*: no information given on publications or aims and objectives of Society *Enquiries*: Richard R. Seidel, at above address

CHESTERTON:
THE CHESTERTON SOCIETY

20 Croft Gardens, Ruislip *President*: John Sullivan *Hon. Sec.*: Henry Reed, Top Meadow, Grove Road, Beaconsfield, Bucks. HP9 1UR *Other officers*: Bernard Cunningham, B.L. Alan Davidson, PhD *Business Manager*: Peter Cullinane *Publications*: The Chesterton Review, 2 p.a. *Membership*: 1,650, of which 200 are in Britain

Enquiries: Peter Cullinane, 54 Evelegh Road, Farlington, Portsmouth, Hampshire

CHESTERTON SOCIETY
St. Thomas More College, Saskatoon, Saskatchewan, Canada *Note*: No information given on structure, membership or publications *Enquiries*: The Secretary, at above address

CHICAGO: UNIVERSITY OF CHICAGO LIBRARY (see under **Friends**)

CHILDREN:
CHILDREN'S BOOKS HISTORY SOCIETY
c/o 25 Field Way, Hoddesdon, Hertfordshire *Chairman*: Brian Alderson *Hon. Sec.*: Mrs. Pat Garrett *Treasurer*: Mrs. D. Aubrey *Other officers*: D. Crutch, R. Taylor, Miss J.I. Whalley *Publications*: Newsletter, approx. 3 p.a. *Membership*: 90 *Enquiries*: Mrs. Pat Garrett at above address

CHILDREN'S WRITERS' GROUP (see **Soc. of Authors**)

FEDERATION OF CHILDREN'S BOOK GROUPS
6 Cavendish Court, Park Road, Eccleshill, Bradford BD10 8AW *National Secretary*: Brenda Marriott *Publications*: Year Book; booklists and information leaflets; Newsletter, quarterly *Notes*: Federation exists to promote an awareness of the importance of children's literature, principally among parents. Also organises Spring & Autumn conferences. Individual groups organise various functions within their local communities *Enquiries*: Brenda Marriott, at above address

FRIENDS OF THE OSBORNE & LILLIAN H. SMITH COLLECTIONS OF CHILDREN'S BOOKS
(Toronto Public Library) Boys and Girls House, 40 St. George Street, Toronto, Ontario, Canada M5S 2E4 *Patron*: H.R.H. Princess Alexandra (the Hon. Mrs. Angus Ogilvy) *Chairman*: Ralph Greenhill *Hon. Sec. & Treasurer*: Newman Mallon *Executive Committee*: comprises 7 members *Publications*: 4 Newsletters p.a.; 1 Gift Book (facsimile) p.a. *Membership*: 785, which includes members of British branch (Children's Book History Society) *Enquiries*: Mrs. M. Dufek, Sec., at above address

CIVIL SERVICE AUTHORS' SOCIETY (see under **Authors**)

CHILDREN cont'd.

CLASSICAL ASSOCIATION (see under **Antiquities**)

CLAUDEL:

    PAUL CLAUDEL SOCIETY

    c/o Dr. Joan Freilich, 600 W. 111th Street, New York, NY 10025 U.S.A. *Membership*: 68 *Notes*: No information received on structure publications or activities *Enquiries*: The Secretary, at above address

CLEMENTS LIBRARY ASSOCIATES (see under **Friends**)

COMIC:

    ACADEMY OF COMIC ART, FANS & COLLECTORS

    P.O. Box 7499, North End Station, Detroit, Mich. 48202, U.S.A *Membership*: 2,500 *Notes*: No information received on structure or publications *Enquiries*: The Secretary, at above address

    ACADEMY OF COMIC BOOK COLLECTORS

    P.O. Box 7499, North End Station, Detroit, Mich. 48202, U.S.A *Founder*: Jerry G. Bails *Publications*: Newsletter — The Comic Reader, 12 p.a. *Membership*: 2043 *Notes*: Microfilm library for research in the field of American Comic Books *Enquiries*: Jerry Bails at above address

CONFEDERACY: MUSEUM OF THE CONFEDERACY

    1201 East Clay Street, Richmond, Va. 23219, U.S.A. *Director*: Dr. Edward D.C. Campbell, Jr. *Publications*: Occasional newsletters *Membership*: 1,000 *Enquiries*: to above address

CONRAD:

    INTERNATIONAL JOSEPH CONRAD SOCIETY

    McMurry College, Abilene, Texas 79605, U.S.A. *President*: Dr. Edmund A. Bojarski *Hon. Pres.*: Philip Conrad *Chairman U.K.*: Mrs. Juliet McLauchlan *Publications*: I.J.C.S. Newsletter, 4 p.a. *Membership*: 750 *Enquiries*: Mrs. Juliet McLauchlan, The Firs, Stone, Aylesbury, Bucks

CONTEMPORAIN: LE LIVRE CONTEMPORAIN & BIBLIOPHILES FRANCO-SUISSES (see under **Bibliophily**)

CRIME/MYSTERY:

    CRIME WRITER'S ASSOCIATION (see under **Authors**)

    MYSTERY WRITERS OF AMERICA INC. (see under **Authors**)

    SOCIETY OF CONNOISSEURS IN MURDER

    Scotland Yard, Purchase, NY 10577, U.S.A. *Membership*: 60 *Notes*:

No information received on structure or publications *Enquiries*: The Secretary, at above address

CROMWELL ASSOCIATION

Combe Lodge, Ringley Park Avenue, Reigate, Surrey *Chairman*: Trewin Copplestone *Hon. Sec.*: Miss Hilary Platt *Publications*: Newsletter — Cromwelliana, 1 p.a. *Membership*: over 300 *Enquiries*: Hon. Sec., at above address

CYMDEITHAS BOB OWEN (see under **Owen**)

CYMDEITHAS EMYNAU CYMRU (see under **Welsh Interest**)

DANTE:

DANTE SOCIETY OF AMERICA

Boylston Hall, Harvard University, Cambridge, Mass. 02138, U.S.A. *Membership*: 425 *Notes*: No information received on structure, publications or activities *Enquiries*: The Secretary, at above address

DELTIOLOGISTS OF AMERICA

3709 Gradyville Road, Newtown Square, Pa. 19073, U.S.A. *President*: James L. Lowe *Publications*: Deltiology, a journal for postcard collectors and dealers, 6 p.a. *Membership*: 1,650 *Note*: Please send IRC for information *Enquiries*: James L. Lowe, at above address

DERBY SHAKESPEARE SOCIETY (see under **Shakespeare**)

DERLETH: (see under **Solar Pons**)

DE ROOS SOCIETY (STICHTING DE ROOS)

Stadhuisbrug 5, P.O. Box 38, Utrecht, Holland *President*: Chr. Leeflang *Hon. Sec.*: Hans P. Eenens *Publications*: Various catalogues and books published for members only *Membership*: 175 *Note*: Fine books for members only, some in English, Dutch, French and German *Enquiries*: H.P. Eenens, at above address

DETROIT: BOOK CLUB OF DETROIT (see under **Books/Collecting**)

DEUTSCHE EXLIBRIS GESELLSCHAFT: (see under **Bookplates/Ex Libris**)

DICKENS:

THE DICKENS FELLOWSHIP

The Dickens House, 48 Doughty Street, London WC1N 2LF *President*: Dr. Edward Carpenter, Dean of Westminster *Hon. Sec.*: Alan S. Watts *Publications*: The Dickensian, 3 p.a., Jan., May, Sept. *Membership*: c. 5,000 *Enquiries*: Hon. Sec., at above address

DIME NOVELS: (see **Happy Hours Brotherhood**)

DODGSON: (see **Carroll**)

*Charles Dickens
Age 46 (1812-70)*

DOSTOEVSKY:
INTERNATIONAL DOSTOEVSKY SOCIETY
c/o Prof. Nadine Natov, Dept. Slavic Languages & Literature, George Washington University, Washington D.C. 20006, U.S.A. *Membership*: 75 *Note*: No information received on structure, publications or activities *Enquiries*: The Secretary, at above address

DOYLE: (see under **Sherlock Holmes**)

DRACULA: (see also **Fantasy/S.F.**)
COUNT DRACULA SOCIETY
334 W. 54th St., Los Angeles, Ca. 90037, U.S.A. *President*: Dr. Donald A. Reed *Hon. Sec.*: Gayna Shireen Reed *Publications*: a Newsletter (no further information available) *Membership*: 1,000 *Enquires*: Hon. Sec., at above address

EARLY ENGLISH TEXT SOCIETY: (see under **English**)
EDINBURGH BIBLIOGRAPHICAL SOCIETY (see under **Bibliography**)
EDUCATIONAL WRITERS' GROUP (see **Society of Authors**)
EDWARDIAN STUDIES ASSOCIATION
High Orchard, 125 Markyate Road, Dagenham, Essex *Note*: No infor-

mation supplied on structure, publications or activities *Enquiries*: Eric Ford, at above address

EIGHTEEN NINETIES:

THE EIGHTEEN NINETIES SOCIETY (Incorporating the Francis Thompson Society)
28 Carlingford Road, Hampstead, London NW3 1RX *President*: Brian Reade *Hon. Sec.*: G. Krishnamurti *Publications*: Annual Journal; Makers of the Nineties: a series of publications comprising biographies of hitherto neglected writers and book-illustrators of the 1890s, uncollected works, unpublished works, reprints of extremely scarce and important material. Titles included: 'Owen Seaman', 'John Oliver Hobbes — Mrs. Pearl Craigie' *Membership*: 400 *Note*: Society's activities include lectures, poetry readings and mounting of exhibitions *Enquiries*: Hon. Sec., at above address

EIGHTEENTH CENTURY:

AMERICAN COUNCIL FOR LEARNED SOCIETIES (see **Eighteenth Century: AMSECS**)

AMERICAN SOCIETY FOR 18TH CENTURY STUDIES (Acronym: ASECS)
421 Denney Hall, The Ohio State University, Columbus, Ohio 43210, U.S.A. Affiliated with: International Society for 18thC. Studies and American Council for Learned Societies. *Publications*: 18thC. Studies, quarterly journal; Studies in 18thC. Culture, annual volume; News Circular, quarterly; Directory; Annual Meeting Program *Membership*: c. 1,800 individuals; 100 institutions *Note*: Scholars and others interested in all aspects of the 18thC. Major disciplines of the membership: modern languages & literatures, Classics, History, Religion, Music and Visual Arts, Science, Bibliog. and all related areas. Annual meeting in April *Enquiries*: The Secretary, at above address

INTERNATIONAL SOCIETY FOR 18TH CENTURY STUDIES (see AMSECS)

ELIOT:

THE GEORGE ELIOT FELLOWSHIP
c/o Mrs. K. Adams, 71 Stepping Stones Road, Coventry CV5 8JT *Patron*: The Hon. Mrs. L.C.S. Fitzroy Newdegate, OBE, JP *President*: Mr. Tenniel Evans *Chairman*: A.F. Adams *Vice-Chairman*: Miss H.

ELIOT cont'd.

Webster *Treasurer*: Mrs. A. Reader *Secretary*: Mrs. Kathleen Adams *Vice-Presidents*: 7 *Publications*: The George Eliot Fellowship Review pub. annually, (free to members); three small booklets; 'Those of Us Who Loved Her', the men in G.E.'s life, pub. Autumn 1979 *Membership*: Open to individuals & institutions *Note*: Aims of Society: to honour G.E., to extend her influence and to hold gatherings of those interested in her and her works. Meetings: approx 10 p.a., including lectures, readings, outings. *Enquiries*: Mrs. K. Adams, at above address

ELVES, GNOMES & LITTLE MEN'S S.F. CHOWDER & MARCHING SOCIETY (see under **Fantasy/S.F.**)

EMERSON:

R.W. EMERSON MEMORIAL ASSOCIATION

c/o J.M. Forbes Co. 53 State Street, Room 903, Boston, Mass. 02109, U.S.A. *Notes*: No information received on structure, publications, membership or activities *Enquiries*: The Secretary, at above address

ENGLISH:

EARLY ENGLISH TEXT SOCIETY

c/o Dr. A. Hudson, Lady Margaret Hall, Oxford *President*: Prof. N. Davis *Exec. Sec.*: Dr. A. Hudson *Editorial Sec.*: Dr. P. Gradon *Publications*: one or two books p.a. *Membership*: 1,300 *Enquiries* about membership: in writing only, to Assit. Exec. Sec., Dr. David Howlett, 83 Kingston Road, Oxford

THE ENGLISH ASSOCIATION

1 Priory Gardens, London W4 1TT *President*: 78-79 R.W. Burchfield, CBE; 79-80 John Sparrow, OBE *Chairman*: Professor Roger Sharrock, Ma, BLitt *Secretary*: Lt. Col. R.T. Brain, MC, MA *Hon. Treasurer*: Michael F. Milton, LL.B. *Publications*: Newsletter: English, 3 p.a.; Essays & Studies, 1 p.a.; The Year's Work in English Studies, 1 p.a. *Membership*: 1,500 *Enquiries*: Secretary, at above address

THE ENGLISH COMPANIONS : ÞA ENGLISCAN GESIÞAS

51 Canterbury Road, Folkestone, Kent, CT19 4PG *Heahwita* (High Counsellor): Dr. Bruce Mitchell *Ealdor* (Chairman): Gil Burn *Gerefa* (Secretary): Malcolm Dunstall *Hordere* (Treasurer): Martin Forder *Publications*: Wiþowinde, quarterly magazine free to gesiþas, or £1

annual sub. to Libraries, etc.; contains articles on lit. as well as archaeology, history, etc.; Seo Freolsungboc þæs Teoþan Gemyndæges þara Engliscra Gesiþa (The Book Celebrating the 10th Anniversary of the English Companions); Remembrance in Good Works, an examination of prose translations of King Alfred *Note*: Aims of this non-political fellowship: to bring together all those with a common interest in the manifold aspects of the Old English or Anglo-Saxon period; to promote a wider interest in, knowledge of and affection for all aspects of the Old English or Anglo-Saxon culture, literature and tradition *Enquiries*: Se gerefa (the Secretary) Membership enquiries: Se Ferscipes Getælere (Membership Secretary), at above address

ENGLISH PLACE-NAME SOCIETY
Dept. of English Studies, The University, Nottingham NG7 2RD
President: Professor Dorothy Whitelock, CBE, FBA *Hon. Sec./Hon. Director*: Professor Kenneth Cameron, FBA *Publications*: Journal of the English Place-Name Society and Annual County Volume *Membership*: 650 *Enquiries*: Hon. Sec., at above address

THE QUEEN'S ENGLISH SOCIETY
c/o The Secretary, 2 South Side, Pullborough, Sussex RH20 2DH
President: Group-Capt. A.P. Campbell, CBE *Chairman*: J.W. Clifton, BA, BSc (Oxon) *Secretary*: A.I. Thompson *Hon. Sec. London Branch*: Miss Joan Worth, 46 Sussex Court, Spring Street, London, W.2. *Publications*: Some Common Errors in Spoken English by J.W. Clifton (chairman & founder); Greetings Card; Glossary of Philological Terms (in preparation) *Membership*: 121, open *Note*: a society for people concerned about the decline in the standard of literacy generally, particularly the misuse and mispronounciation of words in the media of press, radio and television; meetings held in Arundel and London; Society is a registered charity

THE ENGLISH ASSOCIATION OF QUEENSLAND
Lyceum Club, 21 Adelaide Street, Brisbane, Queensland, Australia
President: Mrs. B. Draper, BA *Hon. Sec.*: Mrs. Una Mulholland *Patron*: Rev. Brother J.S. Campbell, OBE, CFC, BA, FACE *Other officers*: F. Hills *Membership*: 32 *Enquiries*: Mrs. Una Mulholland, 217 Wickham Terrace, Brisbane

ENGLISH cont'd.

ENGLISH ASSOCIATION — SYDNEY BRANCH
62 Victoria Avenue, Chatswood, N.S.W. 2067, Australia *President*: S.E. Lee, MA *Hon. Sec.*: Mrs. M.M. Lee *Publications*: Southerly (quarterly) A Review of Australian Literature *Membership*: 120 *Enquiries*: Sec., at above address

EPHEMERA:

EPHEMERA SOCIETY
Church House, Lancing Street, London, N.W.1. *Note*: No information supplied on structure, publications, membership or activities *Enquiries*: The Secretary, at above address

PRINTED EPHEMERA SOCIETY
27b Marchmont Road, Edinburgh, EH9 1HY, Scotland *Notes*: No information supplied on structure, publications, membership or activities *Enquiries*: The Secretary, at above address

EXLIBRIS: DEUTSCHE EXLIBRIS-GESELLSCHAFT e.V. (see under **Bookplates/Ex Libris**)

FANTASY/SCIENCE FICTION:

THE BRITISH FANTASY SOCIETY
447a Porters Avenue, Dagenham, Essex RM9 4ND *Secretary*: Brian Mooney *Publications*: regular, illustrated Bulletin; magazine — Dark Horizons *Note*: a society for those interested in any form of Fantasy in lit., films, art, etc. *Enquiries*: Brian Mooney, at above address *U.S.A. Enquiries*: Jonathan Bacon, Box 147, Lamoni, Iowa 50140, U.S.A.

ELVES GNOMES & LITTLE MEN'S S.F. CHOWDER & MARCHING SOCIETY
5967 Greenridge Road, Castro Valley, Ca. 94546, U.S.A. *Note*: No information received on structure, publications or activities *Membership*: 70 *Enquiries*: The Secretary, at above address

LUNARIANS/N.Y. SF SOCIETY
655 Orchard Street, Oradell, N.J. 07649, U.S.A. *Note*: No information received on structure, publications or activities *Membership*: 50 *Enquiries*: F.M. Dietz, at above address

NATIONAL FANTASY FAN FEDERATION
Route 1, Box 364, Heiskell, Tn. 37754, U.S.A. *Note*: No information received on structure, publications or activities *Membership*: 300 *Enquiries*: The Secretary, at above address

SCIENCE FICTION FOUNDATION
North-East London Polytechnic, Longbridge Road, Dagenham, Essex RM8 2AS *President*: Dr. G.S. Brosan (Director of the Polytechnic) *Patron*: Arthur C. Clarke *Chairman*: C. Barren *Hon. Sec.*: K Bowden *Administrator*: Malcolm Edwards *Publications*: Foundation: A Review of Science Fiction, 3 p.a. *Membership*: by invitation only *Note*: Extensive science fiction library may be used by non-members willing to subscribe *Enquiries*: to above address

FEDERATION OF CHILDREN'S BOOK GROUPS (see under **Children**)

FOLIO:

THE FOLIO SOCIETY
202 Great Suffolk Street, London SE1 1PR *Note*: No information available on structure *Publications*: Newsletter — Folio Magazine, 4 p.a.; Publications — 12-20 p.a. *Membership*: 33,000 *Enquiries*: Membership Sec., at above address

FOLIO FINE EDITIONS LTD.
202 Great Suffolk Street, London SE1 1PR *Note*: No information available on structure *Publications*: Occasional mailings; 1 limited edition published p.a., up to 500 copies, price £350. First title 'Bird Paintings of Henry Jones'.

FOLK:

FOLK LORE SOCIETY
c/o University College, Gower Street, London WC1E 6BT *Note*: No information supplied on structure, publications, membership or activities *Enquiries*: The Secretary, at above address

FORENING FOR BOGHAANDVAERK (see under **Books/Collecting**)

FRAENKISCHE BIBLIOPHILENGESELLSCHAFT e.V. (see under **Bibliophily**)

FRIENDS: (see also **Libraries**)

FRIENDS OF THE OSBORNE & LILLIAN H. SMITH COLLECTIONS OF CHILDREN'S BOOKS (see under **Children**)

FRIENDS cont'd.

FRIENDS OF THE LIBRARY
Trinity College, Dublin 2, Ireland *President*: The Provost, Trinity College *Hon. Sec.*: P. Ussher *Hon. Editor*: W.E. Mackey *Hon. Treasurer*: Peter Brown *Publications*: Newsletter — Long Room, at least 1 p.a. *Membership*: c.600 *Enquiries*: Hon. Sec., at above address

FRIENDS OF THE NATIONAL LIBRARIES
c/o British Library, Great Russell Street, London WC1B 3DG *Chairman*: Lord Kenyon *Hon. Sec.*: Sir Edward Warner *Hon. Treasurer*: Roger Ellis *Publications*: The Annual Report *Membership*: 650 *Enquiries*: Hon. Sec., at above address

FRIENDS OF THE UNIVERSITY OF TOLEDO LIBRARIES
The University of Toledo, 2801 W. Bancroft St., Toledo, Ohio 43606, U.S.A. *President*: Theodore Vogt *Hon. Sec.*: Lucille B. Emch, Rare Books Librarian, Univ. Toledo Libraries *Other Officers*: Leslie W. Sheridan, Director, Univ. Toledo Libraries *Publications*: Occasional publications *Membership*: 200 *Enquiries*: Miss Emch, at above address

ASSOCIATES OF THE UNIVERSITY OF VIRGINIA LIBRARY
Alderman Library, University of Virginia, Charlottesville, Va. 22901, U.S.A. *President*: C. Waller Barrett *Hon. Sec.*: Joanne Trent *Publications*: Newsletter — Chapter and Verse, irregularly *Membership*: 709 *Enquiries*: The Sec., at above address

CLEMENTS LIBRARY ASSOCIATES
Clements Library, University of Michigan, Ann Arbor, Mich. 48109, U.S.A. *Chairman*: Robert P. Briggs *Hon. Sec.*: Dr. John C. Dann *Board*: comprises 17 members *Publications*: Newsletter — The Quarto, 4 p.a.; Annual Report; occasional bulletins and exhibit catalogs *Membership*: 500 *Enquiries*: Secretary, at above address

UNIVERSITY OF CHICAGO LIBRARY SOCIETY
1100 East 57th Street, Chicago, Ill. 60637, U.S.A. *President*: Ann Dudley Goldblatt *Chairman — Nominating*: B.J. Stearns *Chairman — Gifts & Allocations*: Julius Lewis *Other officers*: Brenda Shapiro, Publications; Charles Feldstein, Program *Publications*: Newsletter, irregularly; Bulletin, 2 p.a. *Membership*: 740 *Enquiries*: Mrs. Harriet S. Clowes, at above address

FUTURE:

ASSOCIATION INTERNATIONALE FUTURIBLES

55 rue de varenne, 75007 Paris, France *Secretary General & Exec. Dir.*: Hugues de Jouvenel *Chairman*: Philippe de Seynes *Publications*: Futuribles: monthly journal (circ. 4,000); Futur-Informations: newsletter, 8 p.a. (circ. 12,000) *Note*: International Center for information and futures research *Enquiries*: Secretariat, at above address

INSTITUTE FOR 21ST CENTURY STUDIES

c/o Prof. Cogswell, Dept. of English, Keystone College, La Plume, Pa. 18440, U.S.A. *Note*: No information received on structure, publications or activities *Membership*: 400 *Enquiries*: The Secretary, at above address

AMERICAN TEILHARD DE CHARDIN ASSOCIATION (see under **Teilhard**)

TEILHARD CENTRE FOR THE FUTURE OF MAN (see under **Teilhard**)

GENEALOGY: HERALDRY

SOCIETY OF GENEALOGISTS

37 Harrington Gardens, London SW7 4JX *President*: H.R.H. Prince Michael of Kent *Chairman*: B. Fitzgerald-Moore *Sec.*: office vacant *Hon. Treasurer*: A.M. Hawker *Director of Research & Acting Sec.*: A.J. Camp *Librarian*: L.W.L. Edwards *Publications*: Genealogists' Magazine, 4 p.a. (list of others available) *Membership*: 5,000 *Enquiries*: the Secretary, at above address, with s.a.e.

HARLEIAN SOCIETY

Ardon House, Mill Lane, Godalming, Surrey *Chairman*: R.O. Dennys, MVO, OBE, FSA, Somerset Herald of Arms *Hon. Sec.*: J.P. Heming, BA *Hon. Editor*: C.F.H. Evans, MA, FSA *Publications*: books issued at irregular intervals on Genealogy, Family History, Heraldry, Parish Registers, etc. *Enquiries*: Hon. Sec., at above address

THE HERALDRY SOCIETY

28 Museum Street, London WC1A 1LH *President*: The Duke of Norfolk, CB, CBE, MC *Chairman*: J.P. Brooke-Little, MVO, MA, FSA, FHS, Richmond Herald of Arms *Secretary*: Mrs. J.C.G. George *Hon. Treasurer*: L.G. Pierson *Publications*: Newsletters — The Coat

GENEOLOGY, HERALDRY cont'd
of Arms and The Heraldry Gazette, 4 p.a. of each title *Membership*: 1,600 *Enquiries*: The Secretary, at above address

GESELLSCHAFT DER BUCKERFREUNDE ZU HAMBURG (see under **Bibliophily**)

GOUDY:

THE GOUDY SOCIETY

6219 Canadice Hill Road, Springwater, New York, NY 14560, U.S.A. *Chairman*: Mrs. Edna Beilenson *President*: Horace Hart *Secretary*: John Trieste *Treasurer*: Dr. Robert Leslie *Publications*: no information given *Membership*: 200 *Enquiries*: Horace Hart, at above address

GREENAWAY:

KATE GREENAWAY SOCIETY

318 Roosevelt Avenue, Folsom, Pa. 19033, U.S.A. *Note*: no information received on structure, publications or activities *Membership*: 450 *Enquiries*: The Secretary, at above address

GROLIER: THE GROLIER CLUB

47 East 60th Street, New York, NY 10022, U.S.A. *Note*: no information given on structure *Publications*: Newsletter — The Gazette, 2 p.a. *Membership*: 630 *Enquiries*: All enquiries to Librarian, at above address

GUILD OF BOOK WORKERS (see under **Books/Collecting**)

GYPSY:

THE GYPSY LORE SOCIETY

Coutts House, Sandon, Nr. Stafford *President*: Prof. Walter Starkie, CHJ, CBE, DLitt. *Hon. Sec.*: C.A. Beresford-Webb *Publications*: Newsletter — Journal of the Gypsy Lore Society, 2 p.a. *Membership*: 800 *Enquiries*: Secretary, at above address

HAKLUYT SOCIETY (see under **Voyages**)

HANDCRAFT: ASSOCIATION OF HANDCRAFT PRINTERS (N.Z.) (see under **Printing/Typography**)

HAPPY HOURS BROTHERHOOD

87 School Street, Fall River, Mass. 02720, U.S.A. *President*: Ralph F. Cummings *Hon. Sec.*: Edward T. Le Blanc *Publications*: Newsletter — Dime-Novel Roundup, 6 p.a. *Membership*: 381 *Enquiries*: Hon. Sec., at above address

HARDY:

THE THOMAS HARDY SOCIETY LTD.

The Vicarage, Haselbury Plucknett, Crewekerne, Somerset TA18 7PB *President*: The Rt. Hon. Harold Macmillan, OM, FRS *Chairman*: T.R. Wightman *Hon. Sec.*: The Revd. J.M.C. Yates *Publications*: Hardy Newsletter, 4 p.a.; Annual Review; Tour Guides, books and booklets *Membership*: 900 *Enquiries*: The Sec., at above address

HARLEIAN SOCIETY (see under **Genealogy/Heraldry**)

HARRIS: Joel Chandler Harris (see under Uncle **Remus**)

HEGEL:

HEGEL SOCIETY OF AMERICA

Department of Philosophy, Villanova University, Villanova, Pa. 19085, U.S.A. *President*: H.S. Harris, Philosophy Dept., Glendon College, York University, Toronto 12, Ontario, Canada *Treasurer*: Lawrence S. Stepelevich, Villanova University *Publications*: Journal — The Owl of Minerva, quarterly *Membership*: 325 *Enquiries*: The Secretary, at above address

HENTY:

THE HENTY SOCIETY

c/o 60 Painswick Road, Cheltenham, Gloucestershire *President*: The Most. Hon. the Marquess of Bath *Hon. Sec.*: Roy Henty *Publications*: 'The Henty Society Bulletin', ed. Peter Newbolt, 4 p.a.; list of members *Membership*: (international) c.100 *Note*: Aims: to discover and disseminate biographical and bibliographical information about G.A. Henty (1832-1902); to publish articles on these matters, also critical assessments of the man and his work; to compile and publish a new comprehensive Bibliography, now in preparation *Enquiries*: Hon. Sec., at above address

HERALDRY: THE HERALDRY SOCIETY (see under **Genealogy/Heraldry**)

HISTORY:

THE HISTORICAL ASSOCIATION

59a Kennington Park Road, London SE11 4JH *President*: Professor H.R. Loyn, MA, DLitt, FSA *Secretary*: Miss C.M. Povall, BA *Hon. Treasurer*: C.T. Sharp, MA *Hon. Secretary*: H.L. Freakes, BA *Publications*: Newsletter, pamphlet and 2 journals, each 3 p.a. *Membership*: 10,000 *Enquiries*: to above address

MILITARY HISTORICAL SOCIETY (see under **Military**)

HOPKINS:
THE HOPKINS SOCIETY
114 Mount Street, London, W.1. *President*: Professor N.H. MacKenzie *Chairman*: Dr. A. Thomas *Publications*: Hopkins Research Bulletin; annual Hopkins Lecture; annual Hopkins sermon *Membership*: no figure quoted *Enquiries*: The Secretary, at above address

HOUSMAN:
THE HOUSMAN SOCIETY
Bromsgrove Library, Stratford Road, Bromsgrove, Worcs. *President*: N.V. Housman Symons, CIE, MC, JP *Vice-President*: R.E. Symons *Chairman*: J.M.C. Pugh *Secretary*: J. Hunt *Treasurer*: Miss B.E. Barley *Publications*: journal; newsletter and/or occasional papers; reports & review *Membership*: no figure quoted *Note*: a literary Society, founded in 1973, to bring together all those interested in the lives and works of the Housman family, in particular the poet Alfred Edward, his brother Laurence and his sister Clemence *Enquiries*: The Secretary, Ebury House, Romsley, Halesowen, Worcs. B62 0LN

HYMNOLOGY:
CYMDEITHAS EMYNAU CYMRU (see under **Welsh Interest**)

INDEXERS:
THE SOCIETY OF INDEXERS
28 Johns Avenue, London NW4 4EN Professional society for the maintenance and improvement of indexing standards, with a Register of indexers recognised as competent by its Board of Assessors. *Publications*: 'The Indexer', 2 p.a., April & Oct. *Membership*: 650 in 26 countries; also affiliated Societies of Indexers in Australia, Canada, and the U.S.A. *Commissioning indexes*: Enquiries from publishers and others to: The Registrar, Mrs. Elizabeth Wallis, 25 Leyborne Park, Kew Gardens, Surrey, TW9 3HB. All *other enquiries* to The Secretary, J. Ainsworth Gordon, BA, DipEd, at the above address

INSTITUTE OF 21st CENTURY STUDIES (see under **Future**)
INTER-AMERICAN BIBLIOGRAPHICAL & LIBRARY ASSOCIATION (see under **Bibliography**)
INTERNATIONAL DOSTOEVSKY SOCIETY (see under **Dostoevsky**)
INTERNATIONAL NEWSPAPER COLLECTORS CLUB (see under **Newspaper**)

INTERNATIONAL P.E.N. (see under **Authors**)
INTERNATIONAL POETRY CLUB (see under **Poetry**)
INTERNATIONAL POETRY SOCIETY (see under **Poetry**)
INTERNATIONAL WIZARD OF OZ CLUB (see under **Wizard**)
ITALIC HANDWRITING: THE SOCIETY FOR ITALIC HANDWRITING (see under **Calligraphy**)

JEFFERIES:
THE RICHARD JEFFERIES SOCIETY
c/o 6 Chickerell Road, Swindon SN3 2RQ *President*: Prof. W.J. Keith, PhD., MA *Chairman*: Harold E. Adams *Hon. Secretary*: Cyril F. Wright *Hon. Treasurer*: Mrs. M. Gould *Vice-Presidents*: H.E. Adams, F. Davenport, C.F. Wright, M.N. Daniel *Publications*: Numerous reprints from national and county journals of articles on Richard Jefferies; edited transcripts of talks to the Society *Membership*: open, c.300 members in U.K., France, USA, Canada, Australia & New Zealand *Notes*: Aims: to afford opportunities for fellowship among admirers of R.J.; to promote knowledge of his life & works; to maintain interest in, and concern for, places intimately connected with him. Activities: Monthly meetings from Oct. to April, lectures, discussions, readings; occasional visits

JEWISH INTEREST:
JEWISH BOOK COUNCIL
c/o Woburn House, Upper Woburn Place, London WC1H 0EP *Secretary*: David Hackner *Notes*: no further information available on structure, membership or publications. Aims: to promote the reading of books of Jewish interest; book exhibitions annually; occasional small meetings *Enquiries*: The Secretary, at above address

THE JEWISH PUBLICATION SOCIETY OF AMERICA
117 South 17th Street, Phildaelphia, Pa. 19103, U.S.A. *President*: Edward B. Shils *Executive Vice Pres.*: Bernard I. Levinson *Publications*: 15 books p.a. *Enquiries*: Mr. B. Levinson, at above address

THE SOCIETY OF JEWISH BIBLIOPHILES
c/o Hebrew Union College, 3101 Clifton Avenue, Cincinnati, Ohio 45220, U.S.A. *Membership*: 178 *Notes*: This Society is now inactive and therefore can supply no further information; however several publications of interest to Jewish bibliophiles and others are still

*Dr. Samuel Johnson
(1709-84) Age 72*

JEWISH INTEREST cont'd.

available; a list may be obtained on application to the above address

JOHNSON:

THE JOHNSON SOCIETY

Johnson Birthplace Museum, Breadmarket Street, Lichfield, Staffs. *President*: The Very Rev. Dr. E.F. Carpenter *Chairman*: M.M. Hallett, CBE, MSc, FSA *Hon. Sec.*: R.W. White, JP, MA *Publications*: Newsletter — Transactions, 1 p.a. *Membership*: 600 *Enquiries*: Hon. Gen. Sec., at above address

JOHNSON SOCIETY OF LONDON

The Manse, Tower Road, Hindhead, Surrey GU26 6SU *Note*: no information received on structure, publications, membership or activities *Enquiries*: Hon. Sec., Rev. F.M. Hodges-Roper, at above address

THE JOHNSONIANS

1914 Yale Station, New Haven, Conn. 06520, U.S.A. *Note*: The Johnsonians consist of 50 members who meet annually to celebrate the birthday of Samuel Johnson; each year a keepsake is printed and distributed privately; no information available on structure *Enquiries*: S.R. Parks, at above address

JOYCE:

JAMES JOYCE SOCIETY

41 West 47th Street, NY 10036, U.S.A. *Membership*: 350 *Note*: No

John Keats
(1795-1821)
Age 24

information received on structure, publications or activities *Enquiries*: The Secretary, at above address

KEATS: SHELLEY

KEATS-SHELLEY MEMORIAL ASSOCIATION

c/o Hon. Sec., Keats House, Keats Grove, Hampstead, London NW3 2PR *Patron*: Her Majesty Queen Elizabeth The Queen Mother *President*: The Viscount de L'Isle, VC, KG, GCMG, GCVO, PC *Chairman*: Lord Abinger *Hon. Secretary*: Mrs. Christina M. Gee *Publications*: Bulletin of the K.-S.M.A., 1 p.a. *Membership*: Members of the public cannot become members of the Association, but can become Friends. No. of friends: 300 Membership: by invitation only or by payment of £100 for Hon. Life Membership *Enquiries*: to the above address

KEATS-SHELLEY ASSOCIATION OF AMERICA

41 East 42nd Street, Room 815, New York, NY 10017, U.S.A. *President*: Carl H. Pforzheimer, Jr. *Treasurer*: Donald H. Reiman *Publications*: Keats-Shelley Journal, 1 p.a. *Membership*: 800 *Enquiries*: Donald H. Reiman, at above address

KENT & SUSSEX POETRY SOCIETY (see under **Poetry**)

KIERKEGAARD:

SØREN KIERKEGAARD SELSKABET

c/o rector Emanuel Skjoldager, Hanevangen 7, 2730 Herlev, Denmark

KIERKEGAARD cont'd.

Publications: Kierkegaardiana (scholarly treatises) up to 1979: vol. I-X; Søren Kierkegaard Selskabets populœre skrifter, up to 1979: vol. I-XVI *Membership*: 250 *Notes*: no information given on structure; lectures and meetings held *Enquiries*: The Secretary, at above address

KILVERT:

THE KILVERT SOCIETY

c/o 27 Baker's Oak, Lincoln Hill, Ross-on-Wye, Herefordshire *President*: Wynford Vaughan-Thomas, MA *Deputy Pres.*: Frederick Grice, BA *Hon. Treas.*: J.D. Worsey *Assist. Hon. Treas.*: (for subscriptions) Mrs. E.G. Peters *Hon. Secretary*: E.J.C. West *Publications*: 12-page Newsletter, 3 p.a. *Membership*: over 800, worldwide *Notes*: Aims: Society formed in 1948 to foster an interest in the Rev. Francis Kilvert, his work, his diary, and the countryside he loved; Activities: in and around Hereford, services held at churches associated with Kilvert, outings to the areas associated with his diary *Enquiries*: Hon. Sec., at above address

KIPLING:

THE KIPLING SOCIETY

18 Northumberland Avenue, London WC2N 5BJ *President*: Rt. Hon. The Viscount Cobham, KG, PC, GCMG, TD *Chairman*: W.H. Greenwood *Hon. Sec.*: Lt. Col. A.E. Bagwell Purefoy, RA (Ret'd) *Publications*: The Kipling Journal, 4 p.a. *Membership*: 900 *Enquiries*: Hon. Sec., at above address

KIPLING SOCIETY

420 Riverside Drive, No. 12G, New York, NY 10025, U.S.A. Branch of London Society. *Secretary*: Joseph R. Dunlap *Membership*: 200 *Note*: no information given on publications or activities *Enquiries*: Sec., at above address

LAMB:

CHARLES LAMB SOCIETY

Charles Lamb House, 64 Duncan Terrace, London N1 8AG *Hon. Membership Secretary*: Miss Florence Reeves *Note*: no information received on structure, publications, membership, or activities *Enquiries*: to above address

LANGUAGE: (see also under **English**)

MODERN LANGUAGE ASSOCIATION OF AMERICA

62 Fifth Avenue, New York, NY 10011, U.S.A. *President*: Jean A. Perkins 1979; Helen Hennessy Vendler 1980 *Executiuve Director*: Joel Conarroe *Deputy Exec. Director*: Hans Rütimann *Publications*: MLA Newsletter, 6 p.a.; PMLA, 6 p.a.; MLA International Bibliography, annually *Membership*: 30,000 *Enquiries*: Joel Conarroe, at above address

PHILOLOGICAL SOCIETY

c/o Professor R.H. Robins, School of Oriental & African Studies, University of London, London WC1E 7HP *President*: Professor A.M. Davies *Hon. Sec.*: Prof. R.H. Robins *Other officers*: Council of 20 *Publications*: Newsletter — Transactions, 1 p.a. *Membership*: 690 *Enquiries*: Secretary, at above address

QUEEN'S ENGLISH SOCIETY (see under **English**)

LAWRENCE:

THE D.H. LAWRENCE SOCIETY

8a Victoria Street, Eastwood, Notts. *President*: A. Sharpe *Vice-Pres.*: G. Pollinger *Chairman*: N. Kader *Secretary*: J.L. Parkes *Treasurer*: A.R.S. Cooper *Council*: 8 members *Publications*: Journal, annual; Newsletter, 4 p.a. *Membership*: c.150 *Note*: Society formed in 1974 to unite members in a fellowship dedicated to the promotion of Lawrence. Activities: monthly meetings and occasional outings *Enquiries*: J. Leslie Parkes, 18 Primrose Rise, Newthorpe, Notts.

LESSING:

THE LESSING SOCIETY

Dept. of German, (M.L. 372), University of Cincinnati, Cincinnati, Ohio 54221, U.S.A. *President*: Ruth K. Angress *Hon. Sec. & Managing Editor*: Edward P. Harris *Publications*: Newsletter: Notes and Notices, 2 p.a.; annually The Lessing Yearbook *Membership*: 465 *Enquiries*: Hon. Sec., at above address

LEWIS:

WYNDHAM LEWIS SOCIETY

148 Bellahouston Drive, Glasgow, G52 1HL, Scotland *Hon. Sec.*: F. Fitzpatrick *Other officers*: C.J. Fox, editor of newsletter *Publications*: Newsletter — Enemy News, 3 p.a. *Membership*: 95 *Enquiries*: to above address

LIBRARIES: (see also under **Friends**)
   THE LIBRARY ASSOCIATION
   7 Ridgmount Street, London WC1E 7AE *Secretary*: K. Lawrey JP LLB, Barrister-at-law, FCIS *Deputy Secretary*: R. Bowden, MLS ALA *Publications*: L.A. Record, monthly; L.A. Yearbook, annually books, pamphlets, indexes, abstracts, bibliographies *Membership* 24,000 *Note*: aims: to promote the interests of librarians and librarianship in the UK and the world at large; meetings, conferences seminars etc held throughout year centrally and through various branches *Enquiries*: to above address

   CLEMENTS LIBRARY ASSOCIATES (see under **Friends**)
   FRIENDS OF THE NATIONAL LIBRARIES (see under **Friends**)

   INTER-AMERICAN BIBLIOGRAPHICAL & LIBRARY ASSOCIATION (see under **Bibliography**)

LITERATURE: (see also individual authors)
   THE ROYAL SOCIETY OF LITERATURE OF THE U.K.
   1 Hyde Park Gardens, London W2 2LT *Patron*: Her Majesty The Queen *President*: Rt. Hon. Lord Butler *Chairman of Council*: Lord Evans of Hungershall *Publications*: collections of lectures given: Essays by Divers Hands *Membership*: Fellows: 400, elected Members: 300, sponsored by Fellows *Notes*: aims: to sustain all that is best, whether traditional or experimental, in English Letters, and to encourage a catholic appreciation of literature; activities: lectures, poetry readings, discussions held frequently *Enquiries*: The Secrretary, at above address

LINDSAY:
   VACHEL LINDSAY ASSOCIATION
   502 South State Street, Springfield, Ill. 62704, U.S.A. *Membership*: 300 *Note*: no information received on structure, publications or activities *Enquiries*: The Secretary, at above address

LIVERPOOL BIBLIOGRAPHICAL SOCIETY (see under **Bibliography**)
LIVERPOOL SHAKESPEARE SOCIETY (see under **Shakespeare**)
LE LIVRE CONTEMPORAIN & BIBLIOPHILES FRANCO-SUISSES
   (see under **Bibliophily**)

LOCKE:
   LOCKE NEWSLETTER
   Editor: Roland Hall, Dept. of Philosophy, University of York,

John Locke (1632-1704)

Heslington, York, YO1 5DD *Note*: 10th annual issue, available free of charge to Locke scholars; anyone with a serious interest in Locke can obtain the journal by writing to Mr. Hall. Work of any length is considered for the Newsletter, including articles and notes on any aspect of J.L.'s work or life, or on related authors. Queries are accepted about points in Locke, or unsolved problems; reports on work in progress are published, also reports of discovery of books which belonged to his library; corrections to published works on Locke; also contains a section on recent publications and addenda to previous bibliog. work; book reviews are included when available

LONDON:

LONDON MEDIEVAL SOCIETY (see under **Medieval**)

LONDON RECORD SOCIETY

c/o Institute of Historical Research, Senate House, London WC1E 7HU *Chairman*: Sir Robert Somerville, KCVO *Hon. Sec.*: Heather Creaton *Hon. General Editor*: William Kellaway *Publications* Annual series of hitherto unpublished source material on London history *Membership*: c.350 *Enquiries*: Hon. Sec., at above address

LONDON TOPOGRAPHICAL SOCIETY

Hamilton's, Kilmersdon, Nr. Bath, Somerset *Chairman*: Peter Jackson *Hon. Sec.*: Stephen Marks *Hon. Treasurer*: Anthony Cooper *Hon. Editor*: Mrs. Ann Saunders *Publications Sec.*: Patrick Frazer *Publications*: Principal pub.: facsimile of map, plan or view, or research on topography of London; annual issue to members; in addition: News-

LONDON cont'd.

letter, 2 p.a. *Membership*: c. 500 *Enquiries*: Stephen Marks, at above address

SOCIETY OF ANTIQUARIES OF LONDON (see under **Antiquaries**)
LONG ISLAND BOOK COLLECTORS (see under **Books/Collecting**)
LOST KNOWLEDGE: (see under **RILKO**)
LUNARIANS/N.Y. SF SOCIETY (see under **Fantasy/S.F.**)

MACHEN:

ARTHUR MACHEN SOCIETY

Thomas Library, Wittenberg University, Springfield, Ohio 45501, U.S.A. *President*: Bob Lee Mowery, Director of Libraries, Wittenberg Univ. *Hon. Sec. for USA*: Adrian Goldstone, 35 Lee St. Rd., Mill Valley, Ca., U.S.A. *Hon. Sec. for Great Britain*: W. John Collett, FLA, Central Public Library, Newport, Mon., Wales *Publications*: Newsletter — The Arthur Machen Society Occasional, irregularly *Membership*: 150 *Enquiries*: President, at above address

MALONE:

MALONE SOCIETY

c/o Hon. Secretary, Miss K.M. Lea, 2 Church Street, Beckley, Oxford *President*: Professor G.E. Bentley, 22 McCosh Hall, Princeton, N.J. 08540, U.S.A. *Chairman*: John Buxton, New College, Oxford *Hon. Sec.*: Miss K.M. Lea *Publications*: 1 or 2 volumes p.a. *Membership*: c. 700 *Enquiries*: Hon. Sec., at above address

MALRAUX:

MALRAUX SOCIETY

Box 3231, University of Wyoming, Laramie, Wyoming 82071, U.S.A. *Hon. President*: Marcel Arland, Academie Française *Exec. Secretary & Founder*: Prof. Walter G. Langlois *Publications*: Melanges Malraux Miscellany, semiannual; Serie Andre Malraux (Yearbook), annual *Membership*: 300 *Notes*: Founded in 1969 for persons interested in life and writings of Andre Malraux, French novelist and art critic; Prof. Langlois coordinates research activities relating to Malraux and is organising a Malraux archive *Enquiries*: Prof. Langlois, at above address

MANUSCRIPT:

THE MANUSCRIPT SOCIETY

1206 North Stoneman Avenue, No. 15, Alhambra, Ca. 91801, U.S.A.

President: Barbara McCrimmon *Exec. Secretary*: Audrey Arellanes *Publications*: 'Manuscripts', 4 p.a. *Membership*: 1,250 *Enquiries*: Exec. Sec., at above address

MARLOWE:

THE MARLOWE SOCIETY

193 White Horse Hill, Chislehurst, Kent *President*: Hugh Ross Williamson *Chairman*: Clifford W. Russell, FRSA, at above address *Joint Hon. Secs.*: Mr. & Mrs. G. Capsey, 38 Hilldown Road, Hayes, Bromley, Kent *Publications*: Marlovian Chronicle, irregularly *Enquiries*: Secretaries or Chairman

MARYLAND:

MARYLAND HISTORICAL SOCIETY

201 West Monument Street, Baltimore, Md. 21201, U.S.A. *Director*: Romaine Stec Somerville *Chairman*: J. Fife Symington, Jr. *President*: Leonard C. Crewe, Jr. *Head Librarian*: Larry E. Sullivan *Publications*: Maryland Historical Magazine, 4 p.a.; Maryland Magazine of Genealogy, 2 p.a.; Newsletter: News and Notes, 6 p.a. *Membership*: 6,000 *Enquiries*: Larry E. Sullivan, at above address

MAXIMILIAN-GESELLSCHAFT: (see under **Books/Collecting**)

MEDIEVAL:

EARLY ENGLISH TEXT SOCIETY (see under **English**)

INTERNATIONAL ARTHURIAN SOCIETY (see under **Arthur**)

LONDON MEDIEVAL SOCIETY

University of London, Gower Street, London, W.C.1. *President*: Professor Janet Bately, King's College *Hon. Sec.*: Dr. Dorothy Severin, Westfield College *Treasurer*: Dr. W.F. Ryan, Warburg Institute *Publications*: Medieval Research Students in London, every 2 or 3 years *Membership*: 100 *Enquiries*: D.S. Severin, Spanish Dept., Westfield College, Kidderpore Ave., Hampstead, N.W.3.

SOCIETY FOR THE STUDY OF MEDIEVAL LANGUAGES AND LITERATURE

c/o Hon. Sec., St. Peter's College, Oxford *President*: Professor N. Davis *Hon. Sec.*: R.C.D. Perman *Editor*: Professor J.A.W. Bennett *Publications*: Medium Ævum, 2 p.a. *Membership*: 1,200 *Enquiries*: Hon. Sec., at above address

MELVILLE SOCIETY

Dept. of English, University of Pennsylvania, Philadelphia, Pa. 19104,

*John Milton (1608-74)
Age 59*

MELVILLE cont'd.

U.S.A. *Publications*: Society sponsors publication of Melville Society Extracts, and other scholarly works; Melville Calendar 1975; Mailloux & Parker Checklist of Melville Reviews; 'Moby-Dick' Concordance, 1978 with University Microfilms *Note*: The Melville Society is an organisation of Melville scholars and enthusiasts; founded 1946; holds meetings in conjunction with Modern Language Association (See under Language); conferences every two or three years *Membership*: 600 open *Enquiries*: to above address

MENSA:

BRITISH MENSA SOCIETY

British Mensa Ltd., Bond House, St. John's Square, Wolverhampton *Chairman*: Michael Collier-Bradley *Hon. Sec.*: Barbara Courtney *Publications*: Mensa Newsletter, 10-12 p.a. *Membership*: 2,800 *Enquiries*: Hon. Sec., at above address

MERTON:

THOMAS MERTON FOUNDATION

5 Rosemont Avenue, Farmingville, NY 11738, U.S.A. *Membership*: 127 *Notes*: no information received on structure, publications or activities *Enquiries*: The Secretary, at above address

MILITARY:

MILITARY HISTORICAL SOCIETY

Duke of York's H.Q., London, S.W.3 *President*: Field Marshal Lord Carver, GCB, CBE, DSO, MC *Hon. Sec.*: John Gaylor *Publications*: The Bulletin of the Military Historical Society, 4 p.a. *Membership*: 1,500 *Enquiries*: John Gaylor, 7 East Woodside, Bexley, Kent DA 5 3PG

Sir Thomas More (1478-1535)

MILTON:
MILTON SOCIETY OF AMERICA
English Dept., Duquesne University, Pittsburgh, Pa. 15219, U.S.A. *Publications*: Annual Bulletin *Membership*: 400 *Note*: no further information available on structure, activities, etc. *Enquiries*: Albert C. Labriola, Secretary, at above address
MODERN LANGUAGE ASSOCIATION OF AMERICA (see under **Language**)

MORE:
AMICI THOMAE MORI
B.P. 808, 49005 Angers Cedex, France *President*: Nicolas Barker, The British Library *Vice-President*: Prof. W.S. Allen, Univ. of Alabama *International Secretary*: Prof. Germain Marc 'hadour *Hon. Sec. U.K.*: Rosemary Rendel, 24 Lennox Gardens, London SW1X 0DQ *Publications*: Moreana, bilingual (English-French) quarterly; Thomas-More Gazette, annual *Membership*: 900 *Enquiries*: to above address

MORLEY:
CHRISTOPHER MORLEY KNOTHOLE ASSOCIATION
Bryant Library, Paper Mill Road, Roslyn, L.I., NY 11576, U.S.A. *President*: Herman Abromsom *Curator of the collection*: Marion Altman *Publications*: C.M.K.A. Newsletter, 2 p.a. *Membership*: 168 *Enquiries*: to above address

MORRIS:
WILLIAM MORRIS SOCIETY AND KELMSCOTT FELLOWSHIP
Kelmscott House, 26 Upper Mall, Hammersmith, London W6 9TA *President*: Sir Basil Blackwell *Hon. Sec.*: R.C.H. Briggs *Publications*:

MORRIS cont'd.

Newsletter to members 6 p.a.; Journal and Transactions, both irregular *Membership*: 1,000 worldwide *Enquiries*: The Secretary, at above address

WILLIAM MORRIS SOCIETY

c/o 420 Riverside Drive 12G, New York, NY 10025, U.S.A. Branch of London Society *Secretary*: Joseph R. Dunlap *Publications*: News from Anywhere, an irregular compilation of information and comment; Studies in the Late Romances of Wm. Morris, 1976; The After-Summer Seed (studies in Morris's Sigurd the Volsung), 1979 *Membership*: 340 *Enquiries*: Sec., at above address

MURDER:

SOCIETY OF CONNOISSEURS IN MURDER (see under **Crime**)
MUSEUM OF CONFEDERACY (see under **Confederacy**)
MYSTERY WRITERS OF AMERICA INC. (see under **Authors**)

NATIONAL BOOK LEAGUE: (see under **Books/Collecting**)
NATIONAL FANTASY FAN FEDERATION (see under **Fantasy/S.F.**)
NATURAL HISTORY:

SOCIETY FOR THE BIBLIOGRAPHY OF NATURAL HISTORY
British Museum (Natural History), London SW7 5BD *President*: D.E. Allen *Hon. Sec.*: J. Thackray *Treasurer*: A.P. Harvey *Publications*: Journal of the Society for the Bibliography of Natural History, 2 p.a. *Membership*: 550 *Enquiries*: Hon. Sec., at above address

NESPA: NEW ENGLAND SMALL PRESS ASSOCIATION (see under **Amateur/Small Presses**)

NEWSPAPERS:

INTERNATIONAL NEWSPAPER COLLECTORS CLUB
P.O. Box 7271, Phoenix, Arizona, U.S.A. *Secretary*: C.J. Smith *Note*: no further information received on structure, publications, membership or activities *Enquiries*: Sec., at above address

NEW YORK SHAVIANS (see under **Shaw**)

NIN:

ANAIS NIN CIRCLE
Publications Committee, Ohio State University Libraries, 1858 Neil Avenue Mall, Columbus, Ohio 43210, U.S.A. *Note*: an informal group; no further information given on structure *Publications*: include Under the Sign Pisces, Anais Nin and Her Circle; *Note*:

Valhalla 5 — Networks, special Anais Nin issue incl. 39 contribs., i.e. Henry Miller, Sharon Spencer etc. may be obtained from editor (see below) for $3 *Enquiries*: Rochell Holt Dubois, Editor, Merging Media, 59 Sandra Circle A-3, Westfield, New Jersey 07090

NOCK:

THE NOCKIAN SOCIETY

30 South Broadway, Irvington, New York, NY 10533, U.S.A. *Hon. Sec.*: Edmund A. Opitz *Publications*: Newsletter — occasional memorandum, 2 p.a. *Membership*: 600 *Note*: a Society for people intrigued by Albert Jay Nock, 1870-1945, American editor, essayist, biographer; the Society keeps out of its members' way, as it pursues a policy of salutary neglect *Enquiries*: to above address

NOTTINGHAM SHAKESPEARE SOCIETY (see under **Shakespeare**)

OLD WATER COLOUR SOCIETY'S CLUB (see under **Water Colour**)

OWEN:

CYMDEITHAS BOB OWEN

Tresalem, Pontyberem, Dyfed, S. Wales *President*: Dr. E.D. Jones *Chairman*: D. Tecwyn Lloyd *Hon. Sec.*: Parchedig Dafydd Wyn Wiliam *Publications*: Newsletter — Y Casglwr, 3 p.a. *Membership*: 350 *Enquiries*: Hon. Sec., at above address

OXFORD ANTIQUE COLLECTORS CLUB (see under **Antiquities/ Antiques**)

OXFORD BIBLIOGRAPHICAL SOCIETY (see under **Bibliography**)

OXFORD BOOK ASSOCIATION (see under **Books/Collecting**)

OZ: INTERNATIONAL WIZARD OF OZ CLUB (see under **Wizard**)

PAINE:

THOMAS PAINE SOCIETY

43 Eugene Gardens, Nottingham NG2 3LF *President*: The Rt. Hon. Michael Foot, MP *Chairman*: Christopher Brunel, ARPS *Vice-Pres.*: W.W. Hamilton, MP, Jesse Collins, F.A. Ridley, Prof. A.O. Aldridge, Mrs. O.B. Pell, Audrey Williamson, The Hon. Paul O'Dwyer, Dr. Gary De Young *Secretary*: R.W. Morrell, FLS, FGS *Other officers*: Council of twelve members *Publications*: Newsletter, 2 p.a.; Bulletin, annual journal of c. 30pp; various folders on Paine *Membership*: UK 250, foreign 173 *Note*: Aims: to develop interest in the life and works of Thomas Paine; Society owns a library containing many rare pubs. on Paine and early edns. of his works, ephemera, prints,

PAINE cont'd.

documents, etc.; this is lodged with the Norfolk County Library and is available for research *Enquiries*: Hon. Sec., at above address

PEAKE:

MERVYN PEAKE SOCIETY

c/o J. Watney, Flat 36, 5 Elm Park Gardens, London SW10 9QQ *President*: Maeve Gilmore *Chairman*: John Watney *Editor*: G.P. Winnington *Publications*: Mervyn Peake Review, 2 p.a., Spring & Autumn *Membership*: 120 *Enquiries*: to above address

PEIRCE:

CHARLES S. PEIRCE SOCIETY

c/o Prof. Peter H. Hare, Philosophy Dept., Baldy Hall, Suny Buffalo, Buffalo, N.Y. 14260, U.S.A. *Note*: no information available on structure *Publications*: Transactions of the Charles S. Peirce Society: a Quarterly Journal in American Philosophy *Membership*: 500 *Enquiries*: Prof. Hare, at above address

PENGUIN:

PENGUIN COLLECTORS' SOCIETY

c/o 12 Hornsey Rise, Islington, London N.19 *Secretary*: R.W. Smith, BA *Publications*: Penguin Collectors' Society Newsletter, 2 p.a. *Membership*: 200 *Enquiries*: Secretary, at above address

PENMAN CLUB (see under **Authors**)

PEOPLE AND PLACES

49 Victoria Street, London SW1H 0EU *Patrons*: Lady Diana Cooper, Sir John Gielgud, CH *Chairman*: Miss Anna Calder-Marshall *Publications*: Newsletter, 2 p.a. *Note*: People and Places holds regular soirees in houses or venues in which famous hostesses, writers, poets or musicians once lived or visited, where their own poetry, prose, letters and music are read or played by actors and musicians. All proceeds from these soirees are given to Action Research for the Crippled Child. The annual membership sub. entitles members to advance mailing of recitals and soirees, a 10% reduction on tickets, and the Newsletters *Enquiries*: membership enquiries and further details from Mrs. Iris Banham-Lee, at the above address

PEPYS:

THE SAMUEL PEPYS CLUB

108 Dulwich Village, London SE21 7AQ *Secretary*: R.H. Adams, TD, MA, FSA *Publications*: Newsletter, 2 p.a.; occasional Papers

Edgar Allan Poe (1809-1849)
Age 39

read by members at meetings of the Club; Vol I 1903-14, pub. '17; Vol II 1917-23, pub. '25; 250 copies only of each volume printed for members; these are now collectors items, but there are a few uncut pp left of Vol. I, which could be bound up; at present a collection is being made of the post-war series of Pepysian papers *Membership*: c.100, open to those with genuine interest in Pepys, who can find a sponsor among present members *Note*: activities include a summer outing, annual dinner and an annual service at the Church of St. Olave, Hart Street, where a paper is read *Enquiries*: the Secretary, at above address

PHILOBIBLON CLUB: (see under **Bibliophily**)

PHILOLOGICAL SOCIETY (see under **Language**)

PITTSBURGH BIBLIOPHILES (see under **Bibliophily**)

PLACE-NAMES: ENGLISH PLACE NAME SOCIETY (see under **English**)

POE:

EDGAR ALLAN POE SOCIETY OF BALTIMORE

c/o Alexander Rose, University of Baltimore, 1430 N. Charles Street, Baltimore, Maryland 21201, U.S.A. *Membership*: 350 *Note*: no information received on structure, publications or activities *Enquiries*: A. Rose, at above address

POETRY:

THE POETRY SOCIETY

21 Earls Court Square, London, S.W.5. *President*: Hugh MacDiarmid *Chairman*: Miss Paddy Kitchen *Gen. Sec.*: Robert Vas Dias *Hon. Treasurer*: Mrs. Vicky Allen *Publications*: Newsletter, every two

POETRY cont'd.

months; The Poetry Review, quarterly *Membership*: c. 1,000 *Enquiries*: Gen. Sec., at above address

POETS' WORKSHOP

c/o 51 Roderick Road, London NW3 2NP *Publications*: Booklet containing new unpublished poems by members, 3 p.a., sent to all members *Membership*: no figure quoted *Note*: Poets' Workshop is the leading poetry discussion group in London; it is the successor of the group founded in 1965. Members include poets, pub. and unpub., critics and anyone with an interest in poetry. Meetings held: Nat. Poetry Centre, 21 Earls' Court Sq., SW5 from Oct. to July, at which a member reads his poems from Society booklet and each is discussed. All types of poetry welcome, but members limited to one reading p.a. *Enquiries*: and further information from James Sutherland-Smith, at above address

INTERNATIONAL POETRY SOCIETY

Rose House, Youlgrave, Bakewell, Derbyshire *Director*: Robin Gregory *Publications*: Orbis; Ipse *Membership*: 900 *Enquiries*: Robin Gregory, at above address

KENT AND SUSSEX POETRY SOCIETY

Church House, 1 Ferndale, Tunbridge Wells, Kent *President*: Laurence Lerner *Chairman*: Dr. Gordon Wallace *Hon. Sec.*: Mrs. Iris Munns *Publications*: Newsleter: 'Folio' — Members' poetry published annually *Membership*: 50 *Enquiries*: Mrs. Munns, 40 St. James Road, Tunbridge Wells, Kent TN1 2JZ

REGIONAL POETRY SOCIETIES

There are a number of local poetry groups in existence throughout Britain, with membership ranging from 40-250, from whom we have received no details for inclusion in this publication.

POLISH INTEREST:

STOWARZYSZENIE AUTOROW ZAIKS (see under **Authors**)

POSTCARDS: DELTIOLOGISTS OF AMERICA (see under **Deltiology**)

POWYS:

THE POWYS SOCIETY

8 Clarendon Street, Cambridge CB1 1JU *President*: Angus Wilson *Chairman*: Glen Cavaliero *Hon. Sec.*: T.D. Stephens *Treasurer*:

John Cowper Powys
(1872-1963)

Martin Branfield *Publications*: Occasional Newsletter; Powys papers read at meetings; The Powys Review *Membership*: c. 120 *Enquiries*: The Sec., at above address

PRAED STREET IRREGULARS: (see under **Solar Pons**)

PRINTING/TYPOGRAPHY:

AMERICAN PRINTING HISTORY ASSOCIATION
P.O. Box 4922, Grand Centrral Station, New York, NY 10017, U.S.A. *President*: Prof. Catherine Tyler Brody *Hon. Sec.*: Ms. Jean Peters *Vice Pres.*: Philip Grushkin, Jack Golden, E.H. Taylor *Treasurer*: Mary Ahearn *Publications*: Newsletter: The APHA Letter, 6 p.a.; Journal: Printing History, 2 p.a. *Membership*: 900 *Enquiries*: to above address

ASSOCIATION OF HANDCRAFT PRINTERS (N.Z.)
34 Waiuta Street, Titahi Bay, Wellington, New Zealand *President*: Philip J. Parr *Publications*: Co-Operative Journal 'Vinculum', 2 p.a.; Newsletter, c. 2 p.a. *Membership*: 65 *Enquiries*: to above address

BERLINER TYPOGRAPHISCHE GESELLSCHAFT e.V.
1 Berlin 61, Heimstrasse 21, Germany *President*: Kurt Wittenbecher, Fritz-Erler-Allee 4, D-1 Berlin 47 *Hon. Sec.*: siehe beiliegendes Mitglieder-Verzeichnis *Geschaftsfurer*: Oskar Pietsch, Heimstrasse 21, D-1, Berlin 61 *Publications*: Newsletter: Vierteljahrlich erscheinendes 'Nachrichtenblatt' *Membership*: 340 *Enquiries*: Oskar Pietsch, at above address

BRITISH PRINTING SOCIETY
BM/ISPA, London, W.C.1. *President*: Alfred Lubran *Hon. Sec.*:

PRINTING/TYPOGRAPHY cont'd.

Alfred M. Jones, 14 Penrose Avenue West, Bowring Park, Liverpool L14 4BL *Editor*: Reg Allenby *Publications*: Newsletter — The Small Printer, 12 p.a. *Membership*: 900 *Enquiries*: J. Dutton, Membership Sec., 13 Rivington Street, St. Helens, Merseyside WA10 4BL

PRINTING HISTORICAL SOCIETY
St. Bride Institute, Bride Lane, Fleet Street, London, E.C.4. *Chairman*: Michael Turner *Hon. Sec.*: Chris Hicks *Publications*: PHS Newsletter, 4 p.a.; annual Journal *Membership*: 1,000 *Enquiries*: Hon. Membership Sec., at above address

SOCIETY OF PRIVATE PRINTERS
under aegis of P.L.A. *Honorary Secretary*: David Chambers, Ravelston, South View Road, Pinner, Middlesex *Membership*: 50 *Note*: aims: to exchange examples of members' work; qualifications for membership: owner of a private press, and a member of the Private Libraries Association

TYPOPHILES OF NEW YORK INC.
140 Lincoln Road, Brooklyn, NY 11225, U.S.A. *President*: Dr. Robert L. Leslie *Vice Pres.*: Abe Lerner *Secretary & Treasurer*: Catherine T. Brody *Publications*: Chapbooks and Monographs *Membership*: 500 *Enquiries*: Dr. R.L. Leslie, at above address

PRINTED EPHEMERA SOCIETY (see under **Ephemera**)

PRINTS:

PRINT COLLECTORS' CLUB
26 Conduit Street, London W1R 9TA *President*: H.N. Eccleston, OBE, RWS *Hon. Sec.*: Malcolm Fry *Membership*: 300 *Note*: no further information available on publications or activities *Enquiries*: Malcolm Fry, at above address

PRIVATE LIBRARIES ASSOCIATION: (see under **Books/Collecting**)

SOCIETY OF PRIVATE PRINTERS: (c/o PLA, see under **Printing/Typography**)

PROUST:

PROUST RESEARCH ASSOCIATION
Dept. French, Laurence, Kansas 66044, U.S.A. *Membership*: 250 *Note*: no information received on structure, publications or activities *Enquiries*: the Secretary, at above address

PSYWAR SOCIETY
8 Ridgway Road, Barton, Seagrave, Kettering, Northants. NN15 5AH *Hon. Gen. Secretary*: P.H. Robbs *Hon. Editor*: R.G. Auckland, 60 High Street, Sandridge, St. Albans, Herts. AL4 9BZ *Publications*: The Falling Leaf, 4 p.a., for which contributions from members are welcome *Membership*: 150 *Note*: Society is an international association of psychological warfare historians and collectors of aerial propaganda leaflets; activities include regular postal auctions of members' duplicates *Enquiries*: Hon. Gen. Sec., at above address

THE QUEEN'S ENGLISH SOCIETY (see under **English**)

RADIOWRITERS ASSOCIATION (see **Society of Authors**)
READING:
UNITED KINGDOM READING ASSOCIATION
6 Barton Rise, Chilton Polden, Bridgwater, Somerset *President*: Gwen Bray, Grange Bungalow, 11 Abbey Court, Horsforth, Leeds *President Elect*: Dr. John Chapman, Romsley Hill Cottage, Farley Lane, Romsley, Halesowen, W. Midlands *Hon. Gen. Sec.*: Stan Heatlie, 63 Laurel Grove, Sunderland *Hon. Information Officer*: Mrs. Heather Cook *Publications*: Journals: Reading, 3 p.a.; Books in Schools, 2 p.a.; Reading Education – UK, 1 p.a.; Journal of Research in Reading, 2 p.a.; Newsletter, 3 p.a. *Membership*: c.4,000, open to all interested in the teaching of reading – individuals, students, institutions and those overseas *Note*: aims: to encourage the study of reading problems at all levels, to disseminate knowledge helpful in solution of problems relating to reading, to sponsor conferences and meetings to implement the purposes of the Association; activities include an annual Course and Conference on reading; local councils organise meetings and conferences also

REGENCY SOCIETY OF BRIGHTON AND HOVE
38 Prince Regent's Close, Brighton BN2 5JP, Sussex *President*: Sir John Betjeman *Chairman*: Professor John Kingman *Hon. Sec.*: Antony Dale *Publications*: Annual Report *Membership*: 580 *Note*: no information supplied on activities *Enquiries*: Hon. Sec., Antony Dale, at above address

REMUS:
UNCLE REMUS MUSEUM

*King Richard III
(1452-85)*

REMUS cont'd.

Highway 441, Eatonton, Ga. 31024, U.S.A. *Membership*: 60 *Note*: no information received on structure, publications or activities *Enquiries*: the Secretary, at above address

RICHARD III SOCIETY

65 Howard Road, Upminster, Essex RM14 2UE *President*: G.P. Bacon *Chairman*: Jeremy Potter *Hon. Sec.*: Mrs. Phyllis Hester *Publications*: The Ricardian, 4 p.a.; The Ricardian Bulletin, 4 p.a. *Membership*: c. 3,000 *Enquiries*: Hon. Sec., at above address

RICHMOND SHAKESPEARE SOCIETY (see under **Shakespeare**)

RILKO:

RESEARCH INTO LOST KNOWLEDGE ORGANISATION TRUST

36 College Court, Hammersmith, London, W.6. *President Emeritus*: Professor Alexander Thom, DSC, MA, Hon LLD. *Chairman*: Commander G. Mathys RN (Ret'd) *Hon. Sec.*: Mrs. Janette Jackson, MBE *Research Advisor*: Keith Critchlow *Publications*: RILKO Newsletter, 2 p.a.; Glastonbury: A Study in Patterns; Mysteries of Chartres Cathedral etc. *Membership*: 830 *Enquiries*: Mrs. J. Jackson, at above address

ROETHKE:

THEODORE ROETHKE MEMORIAL FOUNDATION

11 W. Hannum Boulevard, Saginaw, Mi. 48602, U.S.A. *Note*: no information received on structure, publications or activities *Enquiries*: The Secretary, at above address

ROSSETTI:
> THE ROSSETTI SOCIETY
> c/o The Stone Gallery, St. Mary's Place, Newcastle Upon Tyne NE1 7AA *Note*: an informal group of Rossetti collectors who met frequently in The Stone Gallery, not a literary bookmen's society as such *Enquiries*: Ronald Marshall, at above address

ROMAN STUDIES:
> SOCIETY FOR THE PROMOTION OF ROMAN STUDIES
> 31-34 Gordon Square, London WC1H 0PP *President*: Prof. A.L.F. River, FSA *Hon. Sec.*: Mrs. M. Bennett *Other officers*: P.R. Odgers, CB, Hon. Treasurer; Mrs. P. Gilbert, BA, Secretary *Publications*: Journal of Roman Studies, 1 p.a.; Britannia, 1 p.a. *Enquiries*: The Secretary, at above address

ROXBURGHE CLUB: (see under **Books/Collecting**)
ROYAL SOCIETY OF LITERATURE (see under **Literature**)

SAYERS:
> DOROTHY L. SAYERS HISTORICAL AND LITERARY SOCIETY
> Roslyn House, Witham, Essex CM8 2AQ *Chairman/Hon. Sec.*: Lt. Col. Ralph L. Clarke MA (Cantab) FRSA *Treasurer*: Paul de Voil, The Grange, Witham *Publications*: Bulletins, 6 p.a.; Proceedings, annually *Membership*: 250 *Note*: aims: to promote the study of the life and works of DLS and to encourage performance of plays and publication of her books; archives: 200 items, apart from book collection *Enquiries*: to the above address

SCIENCE FICTION FOUNDATION: (see under **Fantasy/S.F.**)

SCOTT:
> SIR WALTER SCOTT
> c/o P.C. Millar, Secretary, 37 Queen Street, Edinburgh 2 *Note*: purely a social club, holding 1 dinner per annum

SCOTTISH INTEREST:
> ASSOCIATION FOR SCOTTISH LITERARY STUDIES
> Department of English, University of Aberdeen *President*: Alexander Scott *Hon. Sec.*: Kenneth Buthlay *Treasurer*: David Hewitt *Publications*: annual volume; Scottish Literary Journal, semi-annual; SLJ Supplements, 3 p.a.; occasional Newsletter *Membership*: 750, open to all interested in the languages and literature of Scotland *Note*: the aims of ASLS are to promote the study, teaching and writing of

SCOTTISH INTEREST cont'd.

Scottish literature and to further the study of the languages of Scotland. An important Scottish literary work, otherwise unavailable or o/p, is chosen for publication each year. *Enquiries*: Membership: D. Hewitt, at above address General: K. Buthlay, Dept. of Scottish Lit., Glasgow University

SCOTTISH TEXT SOCIETY

27 George Square, Edinburgh EH8 9LD *Secretary*: Mrs. N. MacQueer *Note*: no information received on structure, publications, membership or activities *Enquiries*: The Sec., at above address

SCRIBES: THE SOCIETY OF SCRIBES & ILLUMINATORS (see under **Calligraphy**)

SELBORNE:

THE SELBORNE SOCIETY LTD.

92 The Heights, Northolt, Middlesex *President*: The Earl of Selborne *Chairman*: Mrs. Pearl Small *Hon. Sec.*: Roy Hall *Publications*: Newsletter, 3 p.a. *Membership*: 400 *Enquiries*: Secretary, at above address

SHAKESPEARE:

THE SHAKESPEARE BIRTHPLACE TRUST

The Shakespeare Centre, Stratford-upon-Avon, CV37 6QW *Chairman of Trustees*: Dennis L. Flower, MA *Director & Secretary*: Dr. Levi Fox, OBE, DL *Note*: This Trust is not like most of the Societies listed, it is a special kind of educational institution of charitable status, constituted by special Act of Parliament. Basically, it exists to do honour to Shakespeare on behalf of the nation. The Trust has conservation responsibilities in the sense that it maintains Shakespeare's Birthplace and other properties as national memorials to the poet. It also maintains library, archive and museum collections and it is one of the Trust's aims to further knowledge of Shakespeare's work and times by undertaking a variety of educational and academic activities. The Trust maintains a publications department and also functions as a bookseller within the area of its speciality

THE SHAKESPEARE CLUB

51 Banbury Road, Stratford-Upon-Avon *President*: George Rylands, CBE, LittD. *Hon. Sec.*: Roger Pringle, MA *Hon. Treasurer*: Mrs. E. McMurdo, MA *Publications*: none *Membership*: c.150, open to anyone interested in Shakespeare's life, work and times *Note*: activities:

usually 8 meetings p.a., plus theatre outings; helping to arrange the Birthday celebrations *Enquiries*: Hon. Sec., at above address

DERBY SHAKESPEARE SOCIETY
Shakespeare House 93 Keddleston Road, Derby *President*: D.G. Gilman *Chairman*: D.P. Potter *Secretary*: Mrs. M.J. Williamson *Membership*: c.150, acting and non-acting members *Note*: This Society is esentially an acting society rather than a reading one. Produces a full scale production at a Festival in Spring each year at Guildhall in Derby; also holds a number of social events throughout the year at Shakespeare House, the HQ. *Enquiries*: Mrs. M.J. Williamson, Sec., 13 Cowley Street, Derby

LIVERPOOL SHAKESPEARE SOCIETY
Secretary: Miss Joan Thompson, 29 Bonsall Road, Liverpool 12 *Note*: no information received on structure, publications, membership or activities

NOTTINGHAM SHAKESPEARE SOCIETY
c/o 11 Aylestone Drive, Aspley, Nottingham *President*: Miss L.L. Lewenz, MA (Oxon), JP *Vice-Pres.*: Prof. H. Davies, MA, JP, George Hagan, John L. Kirk, Miss Nellie Smith *Chairman*: Miss D.M. Freestone, LRAM (Eloc.), LGSM (Eloc.) *Vice-Chairman*: J.R. Sheppard *Hon. Sec.*: G.F. Bond, *Hon. Treas.* M.R. Wakely *Other officers*: Committee, comprising 7 members *Publications:* none *Membership:* c.50 *Note*: objects of Society: the study of the plays of Shakespeare and Elizabethan dramatists by readings and lectures; activities: 2 or 3 functions per month, plus annual Dinner *Enquiries*: The Secretary, at above address

RICHMOND SHAKESPEARE SOCIETY
Secretary: Mary Wallace, 29a South Road, Twickenham, Middlesex *Note*: no information received on structure, publications, membership or activities

THE SHAKESPEAREAN AUTHORSHIP SOCIETY
Secretary: D.W. Thomson Vessey, MA, PhD, FRHist.S, FRA Scot., 10 Uphill Grove, Mill Hill, London NW7 4NJ *Note*: no information received on structure, publications, membership or activities

SHAKESPEARE ASSOCIATION OF AMERICA
Box 6328 Station B., Nashville, Tenn. 37235, U.S.A. *President*: C.L.

SHAKESPEARE cont'd.

Barber *Exec. Sec.*: Ann Jennalie Cook *Publications*: Bulletin *Membership*: 750 *Enquiries*: A.J. Cook, Exec. Sec., at above address

SHAKESPEARE SOCIETY OF AMERICA

1107 N. Kings Road, West Hollywood, Ca. 90069, U.S.A. *Membership*: 1,500 *Note*: no information received on structure, publications or activities *Enquiries*: The Secretary, at above address

SHAKESPEARE OXFORD SOCIETY

918 F. St., N. West, Room 612, Washington, D.C. 20004, U.S.A *Membership*: 125 *Note*: no information received on structure publications or activities *Enquiries*: The Secretary, as above address

SHAW:

THE SHAW SOCIETY

High Orchard, 125 Markyate Road, Dagenham, Essex RM8 2LP *Gen. Secretary*: Eric Ford *Publications*: The Shavian; The Shaw Newsletter *Note*: no further information received *Enquiries*: Sec. at above address

NEW YORK SHAVIANS INC.

Box 3314, Grand Central Station, New York, NY 10017, U.S.A *Founding Editor*: Vera Scriabine *Presidents Emeriti*: Richard A Cordell, Edwin Burr Pettet *Advisory Board*: 4 members *Executive Board* 10 members *Publications*: The Independent Shavian, a journal 3 p.a., containing rare original pieces by Shaw, fugitive items from assorted newspapers, articles written by members, scholars, book & theatre reviews, illustrations and photos, news about members and past lectures *Membership*: c. 150 members, plus over 110 university libraries *Note*: Society formed 1962, consisting of Shaw scholars and fans; activities: meetings 1 per month from Sept. to May; publication of journal devoted to life, works and interests of Shaw, his circle and contemporaries *Enquiries*: Douglas Laurie, Secretary, at above address

SHELLEY: (see under **Keats-Shelley**)

SHERLOCK HOLMES:

SHERLOCK HOLMES SOCIETY OF LONDON

5 Manor Close, Warlingham, Surrey CR3 9SF *Chairman*: C. Prestige, MA *Hon. Sec.*: Captain W.R. Michell, RN (ret'd), JP *Publications*:

Sherlock Holmes Journal, 2 p.a. *Membership*: 600 *Enquiries*: Hon. Sec., at above address

BAKER STREET IRREGULARS
33 Riverside Drive, New York, NY 10023, U.S.A. *Commissionaire*: Julian Wolff, MD *Publications*: The Baker Street Journal, 4 p.a. *Membership*: 2,000 *Enquiries*: Julian Wolff, at above address *Enquiries about Journal:* Fordham University Press, Bronx, NY 10458, U.S.A.

STRANGE OLD BOOK COLLECTORS
Scion Society of the Baker Street Irregulars *Information from*: Lucy Green, 8502 Ahern, Apt. 101, San Antonio, Tx. 78216, U.S.A. or Johnnie L. Rinks, Red Leech Division, P.O.D. 21200, San Antonio, Tx. 78221, U.S.A. *Note*: no further information available on structure, publications, membership or activities

SOCIÉTÉ ROYALE DES BIBLIOPHILES & ICONOPHILES DE BELGIQUE (see under **Bibliophily**)

SOCIÉTÉ DES BIBLIOPHILES BELGES SÉANT À MONS (see under **Bibliophily**)

SOCIETY DES BIBLIOPHILES DE GUYENNE (see under **Bibliophily**)

SOLAR PONS:

PRAED STREET IRREGULARS
P.O. Box 261, Culver City, Ca. 90230, U.S.A. *President*: Anna Lee Payne Norris, Lady Warden of the Pontine Marshes *Chairman*: Sir Alvin F. Germeshausen *Hon. Sec./Exec. Officer*: C.J. Gustafson *Official Photographer*: Dr. Walter J. Daugherty *Publications*: The Pontine Dossier, 1 p.a., *Membership*: 3,500 *Enquiries*: C.J. Gustafson, editor, at above address

SOLAR PONS SOCIETY OF LONDON
15 Berwick Avenue, Chelmsford, Essex *Hon. Sec.*: Roger Johnson, BA, ALA *Publications*: The Pontine Dossier (see *Praed St. Irregulars*) *Membership*: 50 *Note*: no further information available on activities, etc. *Enquiries*: The Secretary, at above address

SØREN KIERKEGAARD SELSKABET (see under **Kierkegaard**)

STEINBECK:

THE STEINBECK SOCIETY OF AMERICA
English Department, Ball State University, Muncie, Indiana 47306, U.S.A. *President*: Dr. Tetsumaro Hayashi *Publications*: Steinbeck

STEINBECK cont'd.

Quarterly, 2 p.a., winter-spring issue and summer-fall issue; Steinbeck Monograph Series, 1 p.a. *Membership*: 450 *Enquiries*: Dr. T. Hayashi's secretary

STERNE

THE LAURENCE STERNE TRUST

Shandy Hall, Coxwold, York *Hon. Secretary*: Kenneth Monkman *Publications*: The Shandean, annual volume devoted to Laurence Sterne and his works, scheduled for Dec. '79. The Annual to be sponsored by Laurence Sterne Trust, University of Florida and University of Central Florida; editors: Kenneth Monkman, Melvyn New of Univ. Florida, J.C.T. Oates of Cambridge University; Shandean will publish primary materials by Sterne and a limited number of critical essays, reviews, notes related to Shandean tradition; all inquiries, submissions and other correspondence to Assist. Ed., Prof. Beth Barnes, Dept. of English, Univ. of Central Florida, Orlando, Florida 32816, U.S.A. *Membership*: no members as such, four Trustees and a Council of 12 *Note*: The Laurence Sterne Trust is a charity recognised by Dept. of Education and Science; it now has a subsidiary (see below) *Enquiries*: Kenneth Monkman, at above address

THE FRIENDS OF SHANDY HALL

a subsidiary society of Laurence Sterne Trust, see above *Hon. Secretary*: Julia Monkman *Note*: Members can enjoy special privileges at Shandy Hall, and also receive an annual newsletter

STEVENSON:

ROBERT LOUIS STEVENSON CLUB

c/o *President*: Lettice Cooper, 95 Canfield Gardens, London NW6 3DY *Note*: Although this society was never formally closed down, the club seems to have come to an end and has had no meetings for over a year

STOWARZYSZENIE AUTORÓW ZAIKS (see under|**Authors**)

STOWE:

THE STOWE-DAY FOUNDATION AND THE STOWE-DAY LIBRARY

77 Forest Street, Hartford, Ct. 06105, U.S.A. *Director*: Joseph S. Van Why *Librarian*: Diana J. Royce *Note*: Stowe-Day Library is named for Harriet Beecher Stowe (Uncle Tom's Cabin), and the

Foundation was established and endowed by her grandniece Katharine Seymour Day. Stowe-Day Library also houses the Library of Mark Twain Memorial. Library holdings: 15,000 volumes, 100,000 MS re. 19thC. Americana, Harriet Beecher Stowe, Mark Twain

STRANGE OLD BOOK COLLECTORS (see under **Sherlock Holmes**)

SURTEES:

THE SURTEES SOCIETY

The Prior's Kitchen, The College, Durham DH1 3EQ *Hon. Secretary*: A.J. Piper *Publications*: Annual cloth-bound volume of original manuscript material relating to northern England *Membership*: 280 *Enquiries*: Hon. Sec., at above address

SWEDENBORG FOUNDATION, INC.

139 East 23rd Street, New York, NY 10010, U.S.A. *President*: Philip M. Alden *Vice-Pres.*: Forster W. Freeman, Jr. *Treasurer*: John R. Seekamp *Exec. Sec.*: T.H. Spiers *Manager*: Darrell Ruhl *Note*: this Foundation is an autonomous publishing body independent of any church organisation. Activities: focused on maintaining a flow of the theological works of Emanuel Swedenborg into the mainstream of religious thought *Enquiries*: Darrell Ruhl, at above address

TEILHARD:

TEILHARD CENTRE FOR FUTURE OF MAN

81 Cromwell Road, London SW7 5BW *Publications*: The Teilhard Review *Note*: main object: to make Teilhard de Chardin's thought more widely accessible and more readily understood; no further information given on structure, membership or activities *Enquiries*: The Secretary, at above address

AMERICAN TEILHARD DE CHARDIN ASSOCIATION

867 Madison Avenue, NY 10021, U.S.A. *Note*: no information supplied on structure, publications, membership or activities *Enquiries*: The Secretary, at above address

TENNYSON:

TENNYSON SOCIETY

Tennyson Research Centre, Central Library, Free School Lane, Lincoln LN2 1EZ *President*: The Lord Tennyson *Chairman*: F.T. Baker, OBE, MA, ALA, FSA *Hon. Sec.*: D.E. Hayward, FLA *Publications*: Tennyson Research Bulletin, 1 p.a.; Monographs; Occasional Papers *Membership*: 600 *Enquiries*: Hon. Sec., at above address

THEATRE:

BRITISH THEATRE ASSOCIATION

9 Fitzroy Square, London W1P 6AE *Patron*: H.M. Queen Elizabeth the Queen Mother *President*: Earl of Bessborough *Chairman*: Clifford Williams *Director*: Walter Lucas *Note*: Reference, Borrowing and Sets Libraries with over 250,000 books; information service available on all aspects of theatre; research facilities; various training courses for amateurs, professionals and young people; *Publications*: Drama illustrated quarterly theatre review *Enquiries*: The Director, at above address

THE SOCIETY FOR THEATRE RESEARCH

14 Woronzow Road, London NW8 6QE *President*: Professor Glynne Wickham *Chairman*: Robert Eddison *Joint Hon. Secs.*: Miss Kathleen Barker, Jack Reading *Hon. Treasurer*: John Pick *Publications*: Theatre Notebook, illus. journal, 3 p.a.; Annual Publication; Occasional Pamphlets and Bulletin *Membership*: no figure given; life individual and corporate membership available *Note*: aims: provides a meeting point for all those interested in the theatre, both history and technique; encourages further research into these subjects and is especially anxious to link it to modern theatre practice; founded 1948; activities: six monthly lecture meetings: Oct.—March, one annual Public Lecture *Enquiries*: J. Reading, at above address

THOMAS:

THE DYLAN THOMAS SOCIETY

c/o 7a Cambridge Park, East Twickenham, Middlesex TW1 2PF *Chairman*: Harvard Gregory, Glyn Rhosyn, King's Cross Lane, South Nutfield, Redhill, RH1 5NG, Surrey *Secretary*: Jane Tremlett, at above address *Vice President*: Aeronwy Ellis, Dylan Thomas daughter, together with Pamela Hansford Johnson, John Malcolm Brinnin, Douglas Cleverdon, Aneurin Talfan Davies, Walford Davies, F.J. Martin Dent, Constantine Fitzgibbon, Daniel Jones, Glyn Jones, Ralph Maud, Stephen Spender, R.S. Thomas, Wynford Vaughan-Thomas, Emlyn Williams, Mervyn Levy *Note*: aims: to promote interest and further understanding of the life and work of Dylan Thomas; activities: monthly meetings, on 1st Monday of each month at Sesame Club, 49 Grosvenor Street, London, W.1., with lectures from various guest speakers; future plans include a newsletter for members, readings from the plays and poems, branches in the U.S.A. and Europe *Enquiries*: The Chairman or Secretary

THOMPSON: (see under **Eighteen-Nineties**)

THOREAU:

THOREAU FELLOWSHIP INC.

English Department, University of Maine, Orono, Maine 04469, U.S.A. *President*: Eliot Porter *Chairman*: Walter Foster, Jr. *Editor of Journal*: Dr. Marie Urbanski, at above address *Publications*: Thoreau Journal Quarterly *Membership*: no figure given *Enquiries*: to above address

THOREAU LYCEUM

156 Belknap Street, Concord, Mass. 01742, U.S.A. *President*: John H. Clymer *Curator*: Mrs. Thomas W. McGrath *Publications*: The Concord Saunterer, 4 p.a. *Membership*: 650 *Enquiries*: Curator, at above address

THE THOREAU SOCIETY INC.

State University College, Geneseo, New York, NY 14454, U.S.A. *Hon. Sec.*: Walter Harding *Publications*: Thoreau Society Bulletin, 4 p.a. *Membership*: 1,200 *Note*: The Thoreau Society is an informal gathering of students and followers of Henry David Thoreau *Enquiries*: Secretary, at above address

TOLKIEN:

THE TOLKIEN SOCIETY

14 Norfolk Avenue, London N15 6JX *Chairman*: J. Simons *President*: Professor J.R.R. Tolkien 'in perpetuo' *Hon. Sec.*: Mrs. J. Yates *Publications*: Bulletin Amon Hen, bi-monthly; journal, Mallorn, at least 1 p.a.; occasional booklets sold separately, not included in sub. *Membership*: c. 600 worldwide, c. 400 in UK, 100 in U.S.A.; no qualifications for membership, though one would be advised to have read The Lord of the Rings! *Note*: aims: to provide focal point for people interested in life and works of Prof. Tolkien; to provide publishing facilities for writers about Tolkien; to establish study centre and library for his works; research facilities are, at present, available by appointment only; to set up local groups where members can meet regularly; Society is a registered charity *Enquiries*: Mrs. J. Yates, at above address. Send SAE for reply, no personal callers.

TOPOGRAPHY: LONDON TOPOGRAPHICAL SOCIETY (see under **London**)

TRANSLATORS ASSOCIATION

(a subsidiary organisation of The Society of Authors)

84 Drayton Gardens, London SW10 9SD *Secretary*: G.D. Astley *Publications*: all T.A. news appears in the quarterly journal of The Society of Authors, The Author *Membership*: c. 280 *Note*: The Translators Association is a subsidiary organisation within the membership of the Society of Authors to deal exclusively with the special problems of translators into the English language; members are entitled to all the benefits and services of the parent Society, which include advice on contracts with publishers and others, legal matters, copyright etc. Society also runs a Retirement Benefits Scheme and there is a group BUPA scheme. Activities: Quarterly meetings are held of the Association's executive committee. The Association is now affiliated to the Fédération Internationale des Traducteurs

TRINITY COLLEGE: FRIENDS OF THE LIBRARY (see under **Friends**)

TWAIN;

MARK TWAIN MEMORIAL

Nook Farm, 351 Farmington Avenue, Hartford, Conn. 06105, U.S.A. *President*: Edward Lane-Reticker *Director*: Dexter B. Peck *Curator*: Wilson H. Faude *Publications*: Mark Twain Newsletter, 4 p.a. *Membership*: 1,000 *Enquiries*: Membership Sec., at above address

MARK TWAIN RESEARCH FOUNDATION

Perry, Mo. 63462, U.S.A. *Membership*: 400 *Note*: no information received on structure, publications or activities *Enquiries*: The Secretary, at above address

MARK TWAIN SOCIETY

Robeson Hall, Rutgers University, Newark, N.J. 07102, U.S.A. *Membership*: 250 *Note*: no information received on structure, publications or activities *Enquiries*: The Secretary, at above address

TYPOPHILES OF NEW YORK INC. (see under **Printing/Typography**)

UNCLE REMUS MUSEUM (see under **Remus**)

UNITED AMATEUR PRESS ASSOCIATION (see under **Amateur Press**)

UNITED KINGDOM READING ASSOCIATION (see under **Reading**)
UNIVERSITY OF CHICAGO LIBRARY SOCIETY (see under **Friends**)

VERGILIAN SOCIETY
c/o Charles P. Twichell, Choate School, Wallingford, Conn. 06492, U.S.A. *President*: Charles L. Babcock, Ohio State University *Hon. Sec.*: Adele Knight *Treasurer*: Charles P. Twichell *Publications*: Vergilius, 1 p.a. *Membership*: 1,500 *Enquiries*: Charles P. Twichell, at above address

VICTORIANA:

THE VICTORIAN SOCIETY
1 Priory Gardens, Bedford Park, London W4 1TT *President*: Sir Nikolaus Pevsner, CBE *Chairman*: Michael Robbins, CBE, MA, FSA *Hon. Sec.*: Miss Hermione Hobhouse *Patron*: HRH The Duke of Gloucester *Publications*: Newsletter, 3 p.a.; Annual, pub. in March; various conference reports, walks and tour notes always available; 'Seven Victorian Architects', ed. Jane Fawcett, pub. Thames & Hudson *Membership*: 3,000 *Enquiries*: The Secretary, Miss Hobhouse, at above address

THE VICTORIAN SOCIETY IN AMERICA
The Atheneum, East Washington Square, Philadelphia, Pa. 19106, U.S.A. *President Emeritus*: Henry-Russell Hitchcock *President*: William J. Murtagh *Vice-Pres.*: six Vice Presidents *Secretary*: George Vaux *Treasurer*: Armand J. Thieblot *Directors*: board of eighteen *Publications*: Nineteenth Century, quarterly journal *Membership*: 2,500 *Enquiries*: to above address

VIKING SOCIETY FOR NORTHERN RESEARCH
University College, Gower Street, London WC1E 6BT *President*: Dr. R.I. Page *Hon. Secs.*: Professor P.G. Foote & Mrs. U. Dronke *Publications*: Newsletter — The Saga-Book, 1 p.a. *Membership*: 600 *Enquiries*: The Sec. of the Society, at the above address

VIRGIL SOCIETY
Dept. of Classics, University of Reading, Reading, Berks. *Hon. Secretary*: F. Robertson *Membership*: 600 *Note*: no information received on publications or activities

VIRGINIA: ASSOCIATES OF THE UNIVERSITY OF VIRGINIA LIBRARY (see under **Friends**)

VOLTAIRE:
VOLTAIRE SOCIETY
1837 N. Azalea Street, Basswood, Okeechobee, Fla. 33472, U.S.A. *President*: Rudolph L. Marchfield *Note*: no information received on publications, membership or activities *Enquiries*: to above address

VOYAGES:
HAKLUYT SOCIETY
c/o British Library, Great Russell Street, London WC1B 3DG *President*: Professor Glyndwr Williams *Hon. Secs.*: Dr. T.E. Armstrong, Scott Polar Research Inst., Cambridge & Prof. E.M.J. Campbell, Dept. of Geography, Birkbeck Coll., Gressey Street, London, N. *Publications*: 100 volumes (Series 1 1847-1898) 149 volumes (Series 2 1899-1978) 42 volumes 'Extra' series *Membership*: 2,100 *Note*: The objects of the Society are to advance education by the publication of records of voyages, travels, naval expeditions and other geographical matter *Enquiries*: the Map Library, at above address

WALLACE:
EDGAR WALLACE SOCIETY
4 Bradmore Road, Oxford OX2 6QW *Organiser*: Miss Penelope Wallace *Publications*: Newsletter, 4 p.a. *Membership*: 450 *Enquiries*: Penelope Wallace, at above address

WALPOLE:
WALPOLE SOCIETY
20 Bloomsbury Square, London WC1A 2NP *President*: Sir Ellis Waterhouse *Chairman*: Professor Peter Murray *Hon. Sec.*: Brian Allen *Treasurer*: Reginald Williams *Publications*: Bi-annual volume *Membership*: 502 *Enquiries*: Hon. Sec., at above address

WATER COLOURS:
THE OLD WATER COLOUR SOCIETY'S CLUB
R.W.S. Galleries, 26 Conduit Street, London W1R 9TA *Chairman*: Ernest Greenwood, PRWS *Hon. Sec.*: Malcolm Fry *Publications*: Annual OWCS *Membership*: 700 *Enquiries*: Malcolm Fry, at above address

WAUGH:
EVELYN WAUGH SOCIETY
c/o English Dept., Nassau Community College, State University of

New York, Garden City, New York, NY 11530, U.S.A. *President*: Dr. Paul A. Doyle *Publications*: Evelyn Waugh Newsletter, 3 p.a.; Annual Bibliography *Membership*: 231 *Note*: aim of Society: designed to stimulate reserach and continue interest in the writings of Evelyn Waugh *Enquiries*: Dr. Paul A. Doyle, at above address

WELLS:

H.G. WELLS SOCIETY

24 Wellin Lane, Edwalton, Nottingham *Chairman*: G. Hay *Hon. Sec.*: J.R. Hammond *Publications*: Newsletter, 4 p.a.; Wellsian, 1 p.a. *Membership*: 100 *Note*: The object of the Society is to promote and encourage an active interest in, and appreciation of the life, work and thought of H.G. Wells *Enquiries*: Hon. Sec., at above address

WELSH INTEREST :

WELSH BIBLIOGRAPHICAL SOCIETY (see under **Bibliography**)

CYMDEITHAS EMYNAU CYMRU

Tresalem, Pontyberem, Dyfed, S. Wales *President*: Dr. E.D. Jones *Hon. Sec.*: Parchedig Dafydd Wyn Wiliam *Publications*: Newsletter — Bwletin, 1 p.a. *Membership*: 350 *Enquiries*: Hon. Sec., at above address

CYMDEITHAS BOB OWEN (see under **Owen**)

WEST COUNTRY WRITERS ASSOCIATION (see under **Authors**)

WHITE: (see under **Selborne**)

WHITMAN:

WALT WHITMAN BIRTHPLACE ASSOCIATION

246 Walt Whitman Road, Huntington Station, New York, NY 11746, U.S.A. *Curator*: Bets Vondrasek *Note*: The Association devotes itself to promoting interest in Whitman's life & work; it has a library; it sponsors publications, lectures, concerts, etc. *Enquiries*: The Curator, at above address

WILLIAMS:

THE CHARLES WILLIAMS SOCIETY

11B Roland Gardens, London, S.W.7. *Chairman*: R.W. Wallis *Hon. Sec.*: The Revd. Dr. B.L. Horne *Publications*: Newsletter, quarterly *Membership*: 120 *Note*: The Charles Williams Society exists to promote interest in, and to provide a means for, the exchange of views and information on the life and work of Charles Williams. Regular society meetings are held in London. Local reading and

WILLIAMS cont'd.

discussion groups have been set up wherever there is sufficient interest *Enquiries*: The General Secretary, at above address

WIZARD: INTERNATIONAL WIZARD OF OZ CLUB

Box 95, Kinderhook, Illinois 62345, U.S.A. *President*: Dick Martin *Hon. Sec.*: Fred M. Meyer *Publications*: The Baum Bugle, 3 p.a., includes scholarly and popular articles about Oz authors, illustrators and other aspects of Oz; Oziana, annual mag. of original fiction and art by club members; Membership Directory, annual; Oz Trading Post, 4 p.a., pubs. in which members may buy, sell, or exchange material; maps of Oz; novels by Ruth Plumly Thompson: Yankee in Oz, and The Enchanted Island of Oz; annual Oz calendar *Membership*: c. 1750 *Note*: Founded in 1957 to bring together people who share an interest in the Land of Oz and work by its creator, L. Frank Baum; aims to help members add to their knowledge and enjoyment of Oz through publications, conventions and medium of exchange; activities include conventions with displays of Baum and Oz material, auctions of books, showings of Oz films etc. *Enquiries*: to the above address

WORDSWORTH:

WORDSWORTH TRUST

Wordsworth Library and Museum, Dove Cottage, Grasmere *Note*: although there is no lit. Society with members, meetings, etc., it is possible to become a Friend of Dove Cottage and to receive the annual newsletter *Enquiries*: to the above address

YORKSHIRE: ASSOCIATION OF YORKSHIRE BOOKMEN (see under **Books/Collecting**)

YOUNG:

THE FRANCIS BRETT YOUNG SOCIETY

Birmingham & Midland Institute, Margaret Street, Birmingham 3 *Chairman*: J. Hunt *Secretary*: A.F. Rankin *Note*: this Society was founded early in 1979 and can give no details of publications or activities as yet *Enquiries*: to The Secretary, 30 Cavendish Drive, West Hagley, Stourbridge, W. Midlands DY9 0LS

BOOK CLUBS

Ancient History Book Club
P.O. Box 19, Swindon, Wilts. Newsletter: The Link, 13 p.a.
Antiques Book Club of Century House Inc.
Watkins Glen, New York 14891 U.S.A. President: Dr G.L. Freeman, Hon Sec. Mrs Marian M. Boyce. Newsletter: 3 p.a.
Arts Book Society
P.O. Box 6, Newton Abbot, Devon. Managing Director: K.G. Davis, Newsletter: Art News, 13 p.a. (One of the Readers Union Group).
Arts Guild
P.O. Box 19, Swindon, Wilts. (A quarterly Book Club). Newsletter: 'Gallery' 4 p.a.
Biography Book Club
P.O. Box 19, Swindon, Wilts. Newsletter: Biography Book Club Review, 13 p.a.
British Heritage Guild
P.O. Box 19, Swindon, Wilts, Magazine: British Heritage Quarterly, 4 p.a.
Book of the Month Club
P.O. Box 19, Swindon, Wilts. Newsletter: Book of the Month Club News, 13 p.a.
The Companion Book Club
Hamlyn Publishing Group. Astronaut House, Hounslow Road, Feltham, Middx. Editor: Julie Mulvany. Newsletter: Companion News, 13 p.a.
Cordon Bleu Cookery
P.O. Box 19, Swindon, Wilts. Continuity series of uniform volumes marketed by mail as a set. Not a club in the accepted sense of the word.
Country Book Club
P.O. Box 6, Newton Abbot, Devon. Managing Director: K.G. Davis, Newsletter: Readers News, 13 p.a.
Craft Book Society
P.O. Box 6, Newton Abbot, Devon, Details as for Arts Book Society. Newsletter: Craft News, 13 p.a.
Country Book Society/Gardeners Book Society
P.O. Box 6, Newton Abbot, Devon. Newsletter: Country and Gardeners News, 13 p.a.
Family Book Club
P.O. Box 19, Swindon, Wilts. Newsletter: Family and Home, 13 p.a.
The Great Books Foundation
307 North Michigan Avenue, Chicago, Ill. 60601 U.S.A. President: Richard P. Dennis. Foundation programme in the Humanities and Junior Great Books.
History Book Club
P.O. Box 19, Swindon, Wilts. Newsletter: History Book Club Review, 13 p.a.
History Guild
P.O. Box 19, Swindon, Wilts. Newsletter: History Guild Chronicle, 13 p.a.
Home and Garden Guild
P.O. Box 19, Swindon, Wilts. Quarterly Book Club. Newsletter: Home and Garden Guild Magazine, 4 p.a.

The Imprint Society
Barre, Massachusetts, U.S.A. Editor in chief: Mrs Jane West. Newsletter: Catalogue 2 p.a.
International Collectors Library
(Mail order reprint book club) Doubleday and Co Inc. Garden City, New York N.Y. U.S.A. Editor: Norman O'Connor.
Kings and Queens of England
P.O. Box 19, Swindon, Wilts. (Continuity series: not a club as such).
Literary Guild
P.O. Box 19, Swindon, Wilts. Newsletter: Literary Guild Review, 13 p.a.
Maritime Book Society
P.O. Box 6, Newton Abbot, Devon. Newsletter: Maritime News, 6 p.a.
Master Storytellers
P.O. Box 19, Swindon, Wilts. Newsletter: Master Storyteller Book News, 13 p.a.
Military Book Society
P.O. Box 19, Swindon, Wilts. Newsletter: MBC Bulletin, 13 p.a.
Military Guild
P.O. Box 19, Swindon, Wilts. Newsletter: Campaign, 4 p.a.
Mystery Guild
P.O. Box 19, Swindon, Wilts. Newsletter: Clues, 13 p.a.
New Fiction Society
196 Shaftsbury Avenue, London, W.C.2. Hon Sec. Stanley Jackson. Magazine: New Fiction, 4 p.a.
The Puffin Club
Penguin Books Ltd. Harmondsworth, Middlesex UB7 ODA. Chairman: Kaye Webb Newsletter: Puffin Post, 4 p.a.
Readers Choice
P.O. Box 19, Swindon, Wilts. Quarterly Book Club. Newsletter: Readers Choice Review, 4 p.a.
Readers Union
P.O. Box 6 Newton Abbot, Devon. Newsletter: Readers News, 12 p.a.
Science Fiction Book Club
P.O. Box 6, Newton Abbot, Devon. Newsletter: Readers News.
SCM Bookclub
56 Bloomsbury Street, London. W.C.1.
Skylark (Children's Book Club)
P.O. Box 19, Swindon, Wilts. Write for details to: BCA Library, 16 Mortimer Street London. W1N 8QX
Sportsmans Bookclub
P.O. Box 6, Newton Abbot, Devon. Newsletter: Readers News, 12 p.a.
World Books
P.O. Box 19, Swindon, Wilts. (Monthly book is a special club reprint edition). Newsletter: World Books Broadsheet, 13 p.a.

LITERARY PERIODICALS & TRADE JOURNALS

American Book Collector
1434 S. Yale Ave., Arlington Heights, Ill., U.S.A. Publisher: Jason A. Nogee. 6 p.a.
American Notes and Queries
225 Culpepper, Lexington, KY. 40502, U.S.A. President: Lawrence S. Thompson. 10 p.a. Membership/Circulation: 1,000
Antiquarian Book Monthly Review
52 St. Clements Street, Oxford OX4 1AG Editor: Julian Bingley. 12 p.a.
Assistant Librarian
Central Library, Southgate, Stevenage, Herts. Editor: Brian C. Arnold. Circulation: 14,000
The Book Collector
3 Bloomsbury Place, London WC1A 2QA. Editor: Nicholas Barker: 4 p.a. Membership/Circulation 2,000+
Book Collectors Market (previously 'Bibliognost')
P.O. Box 50, Cooper Station, New York, NY 10003, U.S.A.
The Bookdealer
Fudge & Co. Ltd., Sardinia House, Sardinia Street, London WC2A 3NW. W.K. Fudge, Barry Shaw. 51 p.a.
The Book Exchange
42-44 Hoe Street, Walthamstow, London E.17. Editor: Jean Duncan. 12 p.a. Circulation: 350
Books and Bookmen
P.O. Box 294, 2-4 Old Pye Street, London SW1P 2LR. Editor: Cis. Amaral. 12 p.a
Books For Your Children
31 Church Street, Haxey, Doncaster, S. Yorks. Editors: Anne Wood, Jean Russell. 4 p.a. Circulation: 33,000
British Book News
65 Davies Street, London W1Y 2AA Editor: Gillian Dickinson. 12 p.a.
Children's Book Newsletter
(The Children's Book Centre) 229 Kensington High Street, London W8 6SA. Managing Director: Robin Baker. 4 p.a. Circulation: 5,000
The Clique Ltd.
75 Worlds End Road, Handsworth Wood, Birmingham B20 2NS. Editor & Managing Director: Margaret M. Pamphilon. 52 p.a., for the secondhand & antiquarian book trade only: free copy on receipt of trade card.
Encounter
59 St. Martin's Lane, London WC2N 4JS. Editors: Melvyn J. Lasky, Anthony Thwaite, 12 p.a.
The Horn Book Magazine

Park Square Building, Boston, Mass. 02116, U.S.A. Editor: Ethel L. Heins. 6 p.a. Circulation: 26,000

The Junior Bookshelf
Marsh Hall, Thurstonland, Huddersfield, Yorks. HD4 6XB. Director & Editor: Miss D.J. Morrell. 6 p.a.

Library Association Record
7 Ridgemount Street, London WC1E 7AE. Editor: R.M. Walter, MA. 12 p.a. Circulation/Membership: 24,000

New Library World
16 Pembridge Road, London, W.11. Editor: Peter Labdon. 12 p.a. Circulation: 1,400

The Private Library
37 Lombardy Drive, Berkhamstead, Herts. Hon. Editor: John Cotton. 4 p.a.

AUTHOR AND SUBJECT CLASSIFICATION

Alcott 5
Alger 5
Amateur & Small Presses 5-6
Ampersand Club 6
Antiquities/Antiques 6
Arcane Order 7
Archives 7
Arlis 7-8
Arthurian 8
Aslib 8
Athenaeum 8-9
Audubon 9
Austen 9
Authors 9-11

Bacon 11
Baker Street 12
Baum 74
Bibliography 12-15
Bibliophily 15-17
Books/Collecting 18-20
Bookplates/Ex Libris 20-21
Booksellers 21
Bostonian 21
Boswell 21
Brontë 22
Browning 23
Burns 23-4
Burroughs 24
Byron 24

Cabell 24
Calligraphy 25
Carroll 25-6
Cartography 26
Cather 26
Catholic 26
Caxton 26
Chesterton 26-7
Children 27
Claudel 28
Comic 28
Confederacy 28
Conrad 28
Crime/Mystery 28-9
Cromwell 29

Dante 29
Deltiology 29
Derleth 65
De Roos 29
Dickens 29

Dime Novels 38
Dodgson 25-6
Dostoevsky 30
Doyle 64-5
Dracula 30

Edwardian Studies 30-31
Eighteen Nineties 31
Eighteenth Century 31
Eliot 31-2
Emerson 32
English 32-4
Ephemera 34

Fantasy/Science Fiction 34-5
Folio 35
Folk Lore 35
Friends (also Libraries) 35-6
Future 37

Genealogy/Heraldry 37-8
Goudy 38
Greenaway 38
Grolier Club 38
Gypsy Lore 38

Hakluyt 72
Happy Hours Brotherhood 38
Hardy 39
Harleian Society 37
Harris 59-60
Hegel 39
Henty 39
Heraldry 37
History 39
Hopkins 40
Housman 40
Hymnology 73

Indexers 40

Jefferies 41
Jewish Interest 41
Johnson 42
Joyce 42

Keats 43
Kierkegaard 43-4
Kilvert 44
Kipling 44

Lamb 44
Language 45

Lawrence 45
Lessing 45
Lewis 45
Libraries 46
Literature 46
Lindsay 46
Locke 46-7
London 47-8
Lost Knowledge 60

Machen 48
Malone 48
Malraux 48
Manuscript 48-9
Marlowe 49
Maryland 49
Medieval 49
Melville 49-50
Mensa 50
Merton 50
Military 50
Milton 51
More 51
Morley 51
Morris 51-2
Murder 52

Natural History 52
Newspapers 52
Nin 52-3
Nock 53

Owen 53
Oz 74

Paine 53-4
Peake 54
Peirce 54
Penguin 54
People & Places 54
Pepys 54-5
Philology/Language 45
Place-Names 33
Poe 55
Poetry 55-6
Polish Interest 56
Postcards/Deltiology 29
Powys 56-7
Praed Street 65
Printing/Typography 57-8
Prints 58
Proust 58
Psywar 59

Reading 59
Regency Society 59
Remus 59-60

Richard III 60
Rilko 60
Roethke 60
Rossetti 61
Roman Studies 61
Roxburghe Club 61

Sayers 61
Science Fiction 34-5
Scott 61
Scottish Interest 61-2
Scribes 25
Selborne 62
Shakespeare 62-4
Shaw 64
Shelley 43
Sherlock Holmes 64-5
Solar Pons 65
Steinbeck 65-6
Sterne 66
Stevenson 66
Stowe 66-7
Surtees 67
Swedenborg 67

Teilhard (de Chardin) 67
Tennyson 67
Theatre 68
Thomas 68-9
Thompson 31
Thoreau 69
Tolkien 69
Topography 47
Translators 70
Twain 70
Typography/Printing 57-8

Vergilian Society 71
Victoriana 71
Viking 71
Virgil 71
Voltaire 72
Voyages 72

Wallace 72
Walpole 72
Water Colours 72
Waugh 72-3
Wells 73
Welsh Interest 73
West Country 73
White 62
Whitman 73
Williams 73-4
Wizard of Oz 74
Wordsworth 74

Young 74